Nightmarish Neighborhood #1

The Lost Village of Kensico

by Eric Pleska

Copyright © 2024 Eric Pleska

WWW.RIGHTONDUDES.COM

WWW.BUCKOUTROAD.COM

CONTENTS

DON'T BE SCARED, BE PREPARED

Proceed with caution. This collection of true stories about a once small farming community in Westchester County, NY, contains possibly disturbing and shocking information. While this easy-to-read nonfiction book is crammed with local offbeat history, there are also tragic tales of treason, cruel crimes, disturbing deaths, eerie events, shocking scandals, bloody war battles, and Westchester's oldest unsolved murder.

 The journey explores this nightmarish neighborhood's history, from its first inhabitants, the Siwanoys, in the 1600s through Kensico, NY's final days in the early 20th century. Along the way, some of the biggest names in American history are thrown into the mix, including Major John Andre and General George Washington, plus numerous former Westchester residents who lived and died in the forgotten farming village.

  If you're easily frightened, you may want to stop now. Otherwise, be prepared to discover what lies under the reservoir that provides drinking water to Westchester County and New York City: the horrific hidden history of the lost village of Kensico.

You've come this far; there's no turning back now.

Established in 1683, Westchester County is a bustling suburban area just north of New York City. The county used to include the NYC borough of The Bronx, which now shares its borders with Westchester's three largest cities: Yonkers, New Rochelle, and Mount Vernon.

Home to over 1 million residents across its 48 municipalities, Westchester County, became the first suburban area of its scale in the world to develop, primarily due to the upper-middle class development of entire communities in the late 19th century and the subsequent rapid population growth. Today, it is the headquarters of many major corporations, including General Foods, IBM, and PepsiCo. It has been home to numerous celebrities, sports stars, and former U.S. Presidents, including John F. Kennedy and Bill Clinton.

The county is the birthplace of F.M. Radio, soft serve ice cream, and many famous fictional characters, including Wonder Woman and Frosty the Snowman. Westchester has served as the fictional setting of several television shows, including *The Dick Van Dyke Show*, *Maude*, and *The Facts of Life*, in addition to being a filming location for a variety of television shows and blockbuster movie scenes, including the iconic Zoltar scenes in *Big,* shot on the Rye Playland amusement park boardwalk, *Catch Me If You Can*, based on the life of resident Frank Abagnale, and *Sleepy Hollow*, based on local author Washington Irving's famous fictional tale set just north of Tarrytown, NY.

Westchester County's iconic Kensico Dam contains as much masonry as some of Egypt's legendary pyramids. Construction of the massive 1,843 by 307-foot structure began over a century ago in 1913. With over 1,500 workers involved, they completed the project three years ahead of schedule in 1917, with over 1 million cubic feet of stone utilized from a nearby quarry on Old Orchard Street. The gigantic local landmark holds back 30 billion gallons of Kensico Reservoir, which provides drinking water to numerous communities in the county and over 8 million residents in New York City.

Today, Kensico Dam Plaza hosts numerous events, including antique shows, concerts, cultural festivals, and its annual Winter Wonderland. Its spacious grounds allow Westchester residents to jog, bike ride, picnic, sunbathe, and enjoy the outdoors.

The engineering marvel of Kensico Dam is fascinating. However, what lies under the reservoir water is perhaps more intriguing—the remains of a forgotten village with some notable history and a reputation for controversy.

1.) THE SACHEM'S CURSE

During the 1600s, a band of the Wappinger Confederacy, the Siwanoys, populated the area now known as North White Plains, Valhalla, and West Harrison, NY. At its peak, under the leadership of Sachem Wampage, the group's territory included most of present-day Westchester County, The Bronx, and a significant part of Connecticut.

This group of hunter-gatherers had a vibrant culture. They engaged in diverse activities such as fishing, farming, painting their faces and bodies for different events, trading furs, and wearing Wampum jewelry and belts to denote their social status.

They relied on canoes made from whitewood trees as their chief mode of transportation. Women wore their hair down, while men either removed all their hair except for a front forelock or sported a mohawk. Men wore two flaps of animal hide around their waist, while women often wore an unsewn wraparound skirt. During colder months, they would wear furs from bears, raccoons, rabbits, and other animals, along with deer-skin stockings and moccasins.

Siwanoy men hunted for deer, bear, turkey, waterfowl, and various animals to provide food for their families. They also fished and gathered assorted shellfish from the Long Island Sound. The men used a variety of weapons, including spears, clubs, bows and arrows, and clubs. Women gathered berries, planted vegetables, and made pottery.

The Siwanoy had many fishing and hunting areas, camps, strongholds, and villages throughout what is now Westchester. They often adorned these areas with their emblem - a strong, howling wolf with a raised front paw. Their homes included dome-shaped wigwams, rock shelters, and longhouses.

There was a large Siwanoy village where Rye Lake is located today. They used a trail called Otter Trail, which ran east to west between the Long Island Sound and the Hudson River. This path crossed Bear Gutter Creek near Wampus Pond in present-day Armonk.

Siwanoy warriors utilized several forts, including one near modern-day Old Orchard Street on the hilltop that became known during the Revolutionary War as Mount Misery. Another large Siwanoy fort stood in modern-day Armonk, which Europeans said looked like a castle. According to legend, that's how "North Castle, NY" got its name. The site of that castle-like fort is now the modern location for the worldwide headquarters of I.B.M.

The arrival of European settlers to the area disrupted the Native Americans' routine life. There were numerous conflicts between The Siwanoy and the White man, including several with a colonial militia led by Captain John Underhill.

Born in England, Underhill migrated to America in 1630 to train a Massachusetts Bay Colony militia and work as a bounty hunter. The 21-year-old quickly gained a reputation for being a master manipulator. Once, a group of Native Americans ambushed a pirate ship and killed its captain, John Stone. Although Underhill had no loyalty to Captain

Stone, who was a rumored cannibal, he used the incident as an excuse to launch a violent revenge attack.

Another time, Underhill convinced the general public that seven Native Americans had killed a pig that belonged to English colonists. After vilifying the Natives, the public viewed Underhill as a hero for arresting and detaining the alleged criminals. Underhill's militia locked three of the Natives in a cellar and brutally murdered them with bayonets. Another three of the detainees had ropes placed around their necks and were dragged by a boat until they drowned. Another had his genitals hacked off with an 18-inch knife, shoved in his mouth, and then placed on a millstone and decapitated.

Underhill gained a feared reputation for his vicious acts of violence against Native Americans in New England, especially the Pequot in Connecticut, whom he murdered several hundred during a late-night ambush where he lit their village on fire.

Despite these heinous acts, the militia captain was a religious man. After his minister, John Wheelwright, and Wheelwright's sister-in-law, religious reformer Anne Hutchinson, were both banished for what locals deemed were unconventional religious views, Underhill left New England and returned to Europe.

A year later in 1638, Willem Kieft was appointed as the Director of New Netherland. He was only 36 years old and had no prior experience or qualifications for the job, but was favored due to his family connections. One of Kieft's goals during his tenure in the area that would later become New York City was to build churches. However, he needed funds to accomplish this, which led to his attempt to impose a tax on Native Americans. This concept failed and resulted in resistance. Kieft formed a council of advisors to address the issue, including Captain John Underhill.

Having spent a year in England writing a book about his Native American slayings and his enjoyment of eating raccoons and squirrels, John Underhill was now in New Netherland in the ear of Director General Willem Kieft.

The pair worked together to coordinate numerous surprise attacks against various Native American groups in the area, killing hundreds. Kieft even offered a bounty of (modern-day $60) per "Indian scalp." He also permitted colonial men to rape and enslave any Native American woman or child.

During this time, Siwanoy territory became hotly contested between Dutch and English colonial interests, leading to bands of the Wappinger engaging in battles. Known as Kieft's War, the combat was primarily motivated by New Netherland Director-General Willem Kieft's disdain for indigenous people and greed for land, which lasted five years and cost the lives of some 1,600 Native Americans.

In 1643, Willem Kieft permitted Captain James Sands to lead a construction crew and build houses on Siwanoy land near modern-day Pelham Bay. Construction continued even after the Siwanoys made the repeated gesture of handing Captain Sands his tools and motioning for him to go away. That August, Sachem Wampage led an attack.

The Siwanoy warriors stampeded into the tiny settlement, prepared to burn every house. After sending numerous warnings, Wampage expected to find the area deserted; however, inside one home, he encountered a family going about their daily life.

The homeowner was Anne Hutchinson. After fleeing New England and, according to rumors, after briefly living in a cave near Armonk, Anne and her family moved into the house constructed by Captain Sands. The Siwanoy warriors seized and scalped Anne, her mother, her husband, her children, and several servants. According to legend, Wampage murdered Anne himself.

According to legend, Hutchinson's nine-year-old daughter Susanna was out picking blueberries during the attack. The Siwanoy warriors found her hidden in the crevice of a nearby glacial boulder known locally as Split Rock.

Allegedly, the Siwanoy spared her life because they were intrigued by her red hair, a feature they had never seen before. Instead of butchering her, they took her captive and renamed her Autumn Leaf. Some historians believe they eventually released the red-haired girl after her extended family paid a ransom, while others suggest she eventually gave birth to Wampage's son, Wampage II.

Outraged, Willem Kieft and Captain John Underhill, who personally knew Anne, vowed revenge.

A year later, in 1644, The Siwanoy and other local Wappingers gathered at a winter village for a celebration called "K'mo'hok ki'coy." Historians later called it The Maple Sugar Dance; others called it a corn festival. The Wappinger Confederacy tried integrating the Siwanoy with other bands, including the Raritan, Wecquaesgeek, Tankiteke, and Ramapo. The village's name, Nanichiestawack, meant "place of safety."

As the full moon shined on the snow-covered village, Underhill ordered 130 mercenaries to surround the perimeter with their swords drawn. Over 100 Native Americans rushed outside from the commotion.

Underhill's crew murdered all of them and hacked their corpses to pieces. Severed heads littered the snowy ground. Next, Underhill and Willem Kieft set fire to the Siwanoy huts, eliminating any chance of escape.

The attacked Native Americans preferred to die by fire than be killed by the Whites, so they sat inside and did not make a single sound. Not one of the several hundred that burned alive screamed. It was one of the greatest mass murders ever to take place on North American soil.

Underhill wrote:

"The scripture declareth women and children must perish with their parents in defense of his actions. We had sufficient light from the word of God for our proceedings!"

Dutch navigator David Pietersz de Vries described Underhill's attacks in his journal:

"Infants were torn from their mother's breasts and hacked to pieces in the presence of their parents, and pieces thrown into the fire."

An estimated 700 perished, making it one of the worst genocidal killings in American history. Despite using the pretext of Anne Hutchinson's murder for the attack, her accused killer, Wampage, was not present at the massacre.

David Pietersz de Vries, who had consistently tried to prevent Willem Kieft from launching attacks against the Native Americans, became outraged. That year, he led a popular uprising against Kieft, which resulted in Kieft's removal from office.

Kieft's replacement, Peter Stuyvesant, was announced later in 1645 but did not arrive in New Netherland until 1647. He came to America on the 600-ton Dutch merchant ship, *The Princess Amelia*. Kieft boarded the same ship for his return to Holland a month later. During the journey, *Princess Amelia* got lost at sea and eventually broke apart off the coast of Wales. Kieft's body was never found.

Meanwhile, Stuyvesant befriended Captain Underhill, making him a member of his advisory committee. The friendship, however, was short-lived. After a few years, Underhill turned against Stuyvesant, accusing him of being a tyrant, and unsuccessfully called for an overthrow of the government. After fighting a losing battle, Underhill eventually retired to Long Island.

David Pietersz de Vries helped organize a peace treaty between the warring Natives and Europeans. Wampage agreed to sign the peace treaty with his former adversaries. The sachem, who went by the alias "Wampus" and later "John White" after converting to Christianity, marked the agreement with his son Wampage II and Siwanoys Katonah, Cockenseco, and Pathungo, who became the group's new leaders after Wampage's death.

 Despite the 1644 massacre being one of the largest mass murders in human history, details about it are limited and often debated, including its location. Traditionally, historians have pinned the site to Pound Ridge, near an old rose quartz mine. In recent years, however, SiwanoyNation.org has suggested the village is now underwater, beneath the surface near Woodsbridge Road at the Muscoot Reservoir near Katonah, NY. A few years ago, a fresh perspective emerged.

 A 2021 article on Westchester news website LoHud.com by David McKay Wilson referenced the theory of a Connecticut historian and author, Missy Wolfe. In her 2012 book, Wolfe theorizes the village's location may have been at "the confluence of the Cross River and Croton River, now submerged by the Kensico Reservoir."

 Despite a depleted population after the massacre, the Siwanoy persevered. Sachem Pathungo's land included parts of White Plains and West Harrison. Nearby, Cockenseco ruled as chieftain to the north and Katonah beyond that.

Between 1683 and 1695, the sachems deeded land to White settlers. The Native Americans may not have fully understood the sales contracts under the White man's law. In some instances, they perhaps thought that they were only giving permission to live, hunt, and farm on the land instead of having to move out. It's possible that both sides thought they were taking advantage of the other.

According to legend, one of Sachem Pathungo's stipulations required the new inhabitants to preserve the land's whitewood trees, which the Siwanoy used for constructing their canoes. However, the new landowners disregarded the agreement after the Siwanoy were forcefully evacuated from their homes around modern-day Buckout Road, Old Orchard Street, and Kensico Dam Plaza. The farmers cut down the trees and often used them as firewood

According to legend, Pathungo and Cockensenco are buried close to each other on a hilltop that overlooks a pond and the lands of their ancestors. However, the tale takes a dark turn as it is said that before Sachem Pathungo's death, he placed an ancient curse on the land in response to the destruction of the sacred trees. The curse predicted uncertain doom for the land's new inhabitants.

2.)GET UP, STAND UP

During the early 18th century, the Siwanoy group, once led by Cockenseco, dispersed, paving the way for Quaker farmers to settle in the area and build their homes. Josiah Quinby, John Chlowell, and John Hallock were among the earliest settlers.

John Hallock created a mill pond by damning the nearby Bear Gutter Creek, situated near present-day IBM headquarters. He then built a sawmill, and the developing town became known as Hallock's Mill.

In March 1757, John Hallock penned his will just a month before his passing. He left instructions for all his estate to be auctioned off, with the proceeds divided among his wife Hannah and their six surviving children. A local man named Mr. Birdsell purchased the sawmill and later resold it to Thomas Wright.

Over time, the village changed its name to reflect the mill's new owners. In 1763, the community was renamed Wright's Mills after brothers Thomas Wright and his brother Reuben. Thomas piloted the former Hallock sawmill in the north, near Armonk, while Reuben operated a new gristmill near the Bronx River, close to modern-day Kensico Dam Plaza. The quiet farming community was, however, soon disturbed by politics.

England felt its rule of the thirteen American colonies was benevolent. It had protected the Americans from the French during the Seven Years' War (1756-1763) and, therefore, felt the Americans should help with finances through taxation.

In the mid-1770s, a patriotic revolution began among former European settlers who desired independence from British rule. As they paid taxes, they demanded the right to be represented in government. However, about one-third of America's population remained loyal to the British Crown.

Tensions rose after news reached the area about British troops attempting to seize weapons from American Patriots in Lexington and Concord, Massachusetts, in April 1775. This news further divided the local area, and people began taking sides.

The Continental Congress met in June 1775 to select its leader. The nominees included founding father John Hancock, former British officer Charles Lee, and former army Major George Washington, whom second cousins Samuel Adams and John Adams nominated. Congress selected Washington because of his previous military experience and the hope that a leader from Virginia could help unite the colonies. However, many citizens had different opinions.

The nearest city to Wright's Mills, White Plains, intensely felt the division. The clashing political views of residents led to two famous watering holes. Oakley's Tavern, owned by the patriotic Isaac Oakley, was a popular spot for local Patriots, while Hatfield's Inn, operated by British loyalist Abraham Hatfield, was frequented by local Tories.

The Hatfield family became infamous for their feud with the McCoy family down south, but in the 1770s, they were feuding with the Oakley family in White Plains.

The Oakleys were an established family in the area that owned a lot of land, including a 122-acre farm that is now part of the grounds of White Plains Hospital. Born in England, Miles Oakley became Westchester's first mayor. His son Miles Junior also became mayor in 1730, and soon after, he opened Oakley's Tavern across the street from the original White Plains Courthouse on Village Street, which was later renamed North Broadway.

Abraham Hatfield's establishment stood on what is now South Broadway by the corner of Maple and Waller Avenues. The Hatfield family originated in Nottinghamshire, England, and immigrated to America from Holland. Hatfields have served and died in every American war, and every generation has had at least one preacher. Tavern owner Abraham Hatfield served as a captain in the Royal Army and refused to sign papers against the British Crown despite other family members joining the patriotic cause.

Lewis Morris regularly led meetings at Oakleys. There, the Patriots advocated for immediate separation and an armed revolt against the British. They appointed deputies to meet with deputies from other counties in New York to elect delegates to the First Continental Congress.

Meanwhile, a few blocks away, Reverend Samuel Seabury regularly led Loyalist gatherings at Hatfield's. He strongly supported the British Crown and opposed the colonists' desire to have a rule by committee. Seabury developed a following from his writings, including a protest pamphlet, Free Thoughts on The Proceedings of the Continental Congress, which Loyalist printer James Rivington published in his newspaper, *The Gazetter*. Over 300 Westchester Tories met at one session at Hatfield's Inn and signed a protest, pledging their allegiance to King George III. Rivington printed the pledge and the names of its signers in the newspaper.

After the protest of White Plains was published, Lewis Morris tracked down all the signers. He found almost half of them were too young or otherwise ineligible for voting, including Morris' 16-year-old sister, Isabella Morris. Captain Abraham Hatfield's brothers Joshua and Gilbert, the latter of whom owned a 150-acre farm in White Plains, including all of what today is Delfino Park on Lake Street and Hatfield Hill on Hall Avenue near Muckle Stone Rock, joined the patriotic cause. Families became separated because of the issues that became the reason for the Revolutionary War.

Isaac Sears, a member of a Secret Society group of Patriots called The Sons of Liberty, led a posse of 75 mounted men on a raid. Among them was Westchester's Isaac Martling, who lost one of his arms during the French-Indian War. The attack destroyed Rivington's printing press and the apprehension of Westchester's Loyalist leaders. Rivington and his family fled to England after the mob burned his house to the ground.

Sears' posse disarmed all the British Loyalists they encountered throughout Westchester, including Reverend Seabury, Judge Jonathan Fowler, and Westchester Mayor Nathan Underhill. The trio had a significant Loyalist influence over the town, resulting in their imprisonment. After their release from jail, Judge Fowler switched sides. He joined a regiment, soon sent north under General Benedict Arnold's command.

Isaac Sears even tried to place the Loyalist governor of New York, William Tryon, under arrest, but George Washington ordered him to be left alone. It wasn't revealed until a year later that Tryon and New York City Mayor David Matthews were secretly conspiring to kidnap General Washington and assassinate his chief officers. One of Washington's bodyguards, Life Guard member Thomas Hickey, was involved in the plot.

While serving a sentence in Bridwell Prison for passing counterfeit money, Hickey bragged to his cellmate, Isaac Ketcham, about the plot. To gain his freedom, Ketcham revealed Hickey's plan to authorities. On June 28, 1776, Hickey was court-martialed and hanged for mutiny and treason. Later it was revealed that Hickey planned on poisoning a plate of peas served at Washington's table at the Samuel Fraunces Tavern in New York City. On July 3, General William Howe's brother, Admiral Richard Howe, arrived in New York City with the British army. Howe placed New York City under martial law. Tryon retained his nominal title as governor but with little power.

On July 4, in Philadelphia, Congress approved The Declaration of Independence. The document officially severed ties between America's 13 colonies and Great Britain and may be the most critical in American history. Less than a week later, on July 9, the fourth Provincial Congress met at the county courthouse, near the modern-day corner of South Broadway and Mitchell Place in White Plains. After the charter was signed, the colony of New York officially became a state. On July 11, Judge John Thomas stood on the courthouse steps in White Plains and read the Declaration of Independence to the public for the first time in New York State.

Despite the feeling of growing patriotism throughout Westchester, the months ahead were rough for General George Washington and the Continental Army. Opposing general William Howe led the British Army to victories at the Battle of Long Island in August, and a month later, they successfully occupied New York City. After this, Washington's army retreated to White Plains.

On October 23, Washington established a command post at the Elijah Miller House in North White Plains and chose a defensive position he fortified with two lines of entrenchment. The trenches, situated on raised terrain, protected on the right by the swampy ground near the Bronx River by Reuben Wright's mill, and with steeper hills further back, such as Mount Misery, overlooking modern-day Old Orchard Street and a large hill near Wright's Mill, as a place of retreat.

Washington's next in command, generals William Heath and Charles Lee, stayed at other local houses in the area, including the home of Gilbert Hatfield, where modern-day Hall Avenue meets Buckout Road. The Continental Army's defense stretched out for three miles. Beyond that, on the right was Chatterton Hill in White Plains, which commanded the plain over which the pursuing British Army would have to advance. Several hundred militia initially occupied Chatterton Hill.

Meanwhile, George Washington had turned local militiaman Jacob Purdy's house on his 132-acre White Plains farm into his new headquarters, where he would stay for a week in late October 1776. An early settler named Samuel Horton originally built the house in 1720 and, in 1730, sold it to Jacob's father, Samuel Purdy.

The title see-sawed from Samuel to several of his sons before Jacob took ownership. Some historians believe this is because some of Samuel's sons were Loyalists who eventually fled to Canada. Jacob resided at the house with his wife, Abigail. Her sister, Sarah Smith, married Reuben Wright. The house stood on Spring Street at the foot of Purdy Hill, then called Dobbs Ferry Road (now the intersection of Park Ave and Church Street). The enormous property spread from the Bronx River Parkway to Main Street and northeast to North Broadway. Today, the house has relocated to 630 Park Ave.

While the British maintained a relatively small army, they employed the services of several elite units, including Scotland's Black Watch, a militia dating back to 1725 that featured some of the country's best fighters. Also on the British side were Robert Roger's Rangers, an unconventional unit that often utilized snowshoes, sleds, and ice skates during winter battles. The Rangers had previously destroyed a native Abenaki village in Quebec and captured the city of Detroit. The British also employed the services of German soldiers called Hessians. German princes saw opportunities to earn some extra income by hiring out their regular army units for service. Their troops entered the British service not as individual soldiers but as entire units.

Following the retreat of George Washington's army to White Plains, British General William Howe landed troops in Westchester County, intending to cut off Washington's escape route. To cover the eastern flank of his army, Howe ordered Rogers' Rangers to seize the village of neighboring Mamaroneck, which the Continental army had abandoned. On October 22, 1776, Colonel Haslet led 750 Patriots to attack the British encampment, but Rogers' Rangers drove them off.

General Howe set up his headquarters on a 58-acre farmhouse in Scarsdale, NY, on the White Plains border. Quaker Jonathan Griffen owned the house, built in 1731. It's still standing today on Mamaroneck Road and recently sold in 2019 for just under $1.5M.

On October 24 and 25, British General Howe's army moved closer from New Rochelle to Scarsdale, where they established a camp covering the eastern bank of the Bronx River. On the morning of October 28, his forces marched toward White Plains, with British troops on the right under General Henry Clinton and Hessian troops on the left under General von Heister.

October 28, 1776, is officially listed as the opening day of the Battle of White Plains. At 10 am, bugles and drums sounded. Howe's forces marched through Scarsdale's roads and byways, preceded by an enforced labor battalion consisting of prisoners and locals who cleared the paths, removed fences, and built bridges for the British army to advance. After a minor clash in Scarsdale, the British and Hessians stormed across the shallow Bronx River and mounted an assault up the steep wooded slopes of Chatterton Hill in White Plains.

Armed with muskets, bayonets, and cannons, the British Army, dressed in red coats with caps, marched in a column led by Sir Henry Clinton. General von Heister led a column of Hessian warriors dressed in blue coats and hats with brass front plates.

General Washington ordered about 1,500 Patriots to try to halt the two columns. They fought hard and delivered steady fire, but they were outclassed by a more experienced army and forced to retreat from one stone wall to another.

The Hessians attacked the left flank, which drove the Americans back. Howe moved his men into the flat land below the hill. A sharp firefight erupted as the Americans tried to disrupt the British advance. According to local lore, Alexander Hamilton is among the Patriots who fired cannons at British and Hessian soldiers as they charged up the hill. Washington had approximately 14,000 soldiers, while Howe had about 14,500.

Washington's army spread out, covering approximately three miles. According to a monument on North Broadway between Clinton Street and Crane Ave, that location was the center of Washington's army. Nearby, Washington had troops on Nethermont Ave overlooking Old Orchard Street in White Plains. The bitter cold the troops endured in the hill's trenches led to the area's name: Mount Misery.

The clash of armies was considered a British victory. There have been various estimates of the number of casualties that took place during the battle. Some estimates are as high as 600, which was more than the population of citizens living in White Plains at the time.

It is not clear what happened to Abraham Hatfield following the war. Despite his son Gilbert fighting on the Patriot side and even hosting General Heath at his White Plains home, Abraham remained loyal to the British Crown. Some historians speculate that Abraham passed away before the end of the war, while others maintain that he fled to Nova Scotia, Canada. Either way, the Hatfield Inn not only ceased its

Loyalist activities after the war but also hosted several famous dinner guests, including Lafayette, Rochambeau, and General George Washington.

 The site of the former tavern became Alexander's Department Store in the 1960s. In the 1990s, the building became The Westchester Pavilion, anchored by a large Borders bookstore. Eventually, Borders and other Pavilion stores like Toys R Us and the Educational Warehouse went out of business, leading to the mini mall's demolition. For years, all that remained was a massive hole in the ground, spanning several city blocks.

 On October 31, 1776, General Washington took advantage of a heavy thunderstorm to stealthily relocate his troops towards Wright's Mill. The nearby Purchase Quaker church doubled as a makeshift hospital for wounded soldiers. The army rested and obtained supplies before they clashed with the British Army a few weeks later at the Battle of Fort Washington, near the north end of Manhattan.

Soon after the clashing armies left Westchester, the Quaker farmers who, nearly a century prior, acquired their land from Native Americans and now lived through a Revolutionary War battle had a new problem to contend with: cowboys.

3.) COWBOYS FROM HELL

After the Battle of White Plains, Westchester County had no systematic campaign, but there was continuous fighting. The Americans, with headquarters at Peekskill in the northern part of the county, maintained a series of posts from the mouth of the Croton River across to the Long Island Sound at Pine's Bridge, Wrights Mills, and at other places where the enemy would be likely to break through and enter the upper part of the county.

With headquarters in New York City, the British maintained a similar line of posts at Kingsbridge, Morrisania, Yonkers, and Eastchester. The middle section of the county, about twenty miles broad, with the Hudson on one side and the Sound on the other, became known as "The Neutral Ground," as the troops of either side did not regularly occupy it. The Americans became known as the "upper" party and the British as the "lower."

New York Governor William Tryon, who previously planned to assassinate George Washington until a prison inmate foiled the plot, came up with another terrorizing idea in 1777. He wrote about it in a letter:

"By Sir William Howe's permission and Dir. Henry Clinton's approbation, I have raised a Troop of Light Horse from the Westchester Militia to consist of Fifty Private en to serve during the Campaign. They care Cantooned between our Lines and the Rebels at White Plains and have taken up several Deserters, for which I give

them a Guinea for each an – which checks the Evil spirit of Desertion. This Troop is truly elite, and their captain, James Delancey, is also the Colonel of the Militia for Westchester County. I have much confidence in them."

A century before the mentioning of Jesse James and The James Gang struck fear; Governor Tryon assembled a different James and a different gang of outlaws causing terror. Nicknamed "The Commander of Cowboys," James DeLancey captained an elite group of 50 Loyalists known as The Westchester Refugees, also called DeLancey's Cowboys.

Dozens of men from Westchester were part of this feared unit, which also meant they knew the area's geography and its residents. Member Nathan Underhill was the former Mayor of Westchester. He had an extensive family history connected to the area, including his great-grandfather, Captain John Underhill, the infamous Native American slayer.

Other members, like Captain Benjamin Ogden of North Castle, may have had personal grudges against the Patriots. In Ogden's case, he described that in 1776, he was deprived of his property, including 270 acres at Cortland Manor and 215 acres in North Castle near Wright's Mill, by the "rebels."

Colonel Isaac Hatfield has a similar story. Despite being a member of a prominent area family, local Patriots demanded he serve in their militia and sign their petition against The Crown. When he refused to join, they fined him. When he refused to pay that fine, they jailed him.

While detained, they raided his farm, taking 18 cattle, four horses, and 50 sheep. Upon release, Hatfield volunteered for the Queen's Rangers, commanding a company in that Loyalist regiment. A year later, he joined DeLancey's Cowboys.

Additional members included members of prominent area families, including Fowler, Gedney, Horton, Ferris, Havilland, Wilson, Hunt, Ford, Purdy, and the infamous Merritt brothers, Thomas and Shubael.

James' uncle Oliver became second in command of the Cowboys. Referred to as "The Outlaw of The Bronx," he had prior experience as a Westchester militia captain, as a member of Rogers' Rangers, and years prior, even aligned with Isaac Sears and the Sons of Liberty. The prominent DeLancey family opposed England's Stamp Act and other efforts to tax the colonies. However, they refused to support armed insurrection against the Crown and thus became Loyalists during the Revolution.

James DeLancey previously served as Westchester Sherriff, starting in 1769. He was the son of the wealthy French merchant Peter DeLancey, who owned much property in Westchester, much of which James inherited after Peter's passing in 1770.

The DeLancey family property included one of the country's most extensive horse racing stables. Fittingly, James owned a horse that was reputed to be the fastest in America. Named *True Briton*, the dark chestnut-colored racehorse was a mixture of the Byerly Turk and Godolphin Arabian breeds. He sired a horse named *Figure*, credited as the first of the highly sought-after Morgan horse breed.

One day in 1776, American scouts spotted *True Briton* standing unguarded in White Plains. They stole and sold him to a man from Massachusetts. After the Patriots stole James' horse, he was out for bloody revenge.

The Cowboys' initial duty was to patrol Westchester as a systematic unit and provide the British Army with supplies and beef cattle. However, the crew dressed in matching green coats, brown leggings, and felt hats soon garnered a reputation as ruthless raiders.

For the citizens of Westchester County, who wanted to remain neutral in the conflict, the Cowboys' actions were a nightmare. They feared that at any moment, the Cowboys would plunder their homes, take all their belongings, and leave them with nothing.

Lawlessness and guerilla warfare occurred between Delancey's Cowboys and anyone they chose to encounter. They specialized in rustling cattle from farms in the area and driving the herds through "The Neutral Ground" toward British forces. They often would use the sound of a cowbell to lure a lone farmer into an ambush. They preyed on easy targets, robbed them, and then moved on. During the conflict, DeLancey's Cowboys conducted numerous raids, stealing more than just cattle; some of these raids included kidnapping and murders.

Despite no longer having the country's fastest horse, James DeLancey and The Cowboys became known for their swift hit-and-run tactics as a unit. On October 16, 1777, they plundered farmers in White Plains, taking 44 barrels of flour, two ox teams, 100 black cattle, and 300 fat sheep and hogs. On another raid near Rye, they captured several members of the opposing army. A few days later, in Connecticut, they took 100 cattle and captured 37 Continental Army and militia troops, which they held hostage. They killed an additional ten soldiers.

 The Cowboys attacked a party of rebels stationed at Byram River, killing eight and taking several prisoners. The Cowboys were so fast in their attack that the Patriots only managed to discharge their cannon twice before The Cowboys seized and destroyed it. During the ambush, a picket guard stationed inside a house shot and killed Cowboy Captain Solomon Fowler. The Cowboys responded by burning the house to the ground, killing its inhabitants.

 Perhaps the most brutally documented attack made by the Cowboys occurred on May 14, 1781, at an army camp near Westchester's Croton River. American Colonel Christopher Greene led the African American 1st Rhode Island Regiment. James DeLancey led an ambush, surprising Greene, Major Ebenezer Flagg, and numerous Black soldiers stationed on the north bank of the Croton River. The Patriots could only fire a few shots from their Davenport House headquarters before being overrun.

 The Cowboys killed several dozen soldiers, including Major Flagg. James DeLancey is said to have slaughtered Colonel Greene himself, and according to one account of the attack, Greene's body was found about a mile away in the woods, hacked to pieces.

Built in 1750, The Davenport House still stands at 648 Croton Heights Road in Yorktown, about 15 miles from the site of Wright's Mill. Near the Davenport House is a mass grave with the remains of an unknown number of Black soldiers from Greene's Rhode Island Regiment.

 The terror wreaked by The Cowboys struck the constant fear from the peaceful Quaker farmers and their families of raids in Wright's Mill. To make matters worse, DeLancey's Cowboys weren't the only roving band of bandits spreading fright and destruction.

4.) MARAUDERS

 General Cortland Skinner commanded an armed Loyalist crew that regularly conducted guerilla operations throughout Westchester. Dressed in green, this lethal band of land pirates became known locally as Skinner's Greens or The Skinners. According to some accounts, they sometimes appeared to be feuding with The Cowboys. However, many speculate that it was strictly a rouse to keep up appearances and fool their unsuspecting victims, especially as their second-in-command was James DeLancey's cousin, Stephen DeLancey.

 Gilbert Thorne became North Castle's first town clerk in 1770 and held that position until 1778. Towards his tenure, The Skinners raided his home near Wright's Mills. His wife Charity was alone in the house and recalled they came into the house, demanding food and drink. Frightened, she obeyed their wishes. According to his writings, the marauders "flung a bag of booty in the corner and began a wild carousel." One of the pieces they confiscated was her rare teapot, a piece very special to her family. She concocted a plan to save the heirloom. Plying the raiders with alcohol, she quickly went to the garden and cut a head of cabbage. Then, when the revelers were not looking, she deftly extracted the precious teapot and put the cabbage in its place. The Skinners shortly later exited with their loot bag and, unbeknownst to them, also a cabbage.

 In early 1777, British Lieutenant General Clinton granted German officer Captain Andreas Emerich (known to some in America as "Andrew Emerick") permission to raise a command. He had previously commanded a small unit, which evolved to become The Guides & Pioneers. That August, almost like a modern-day American sports expansion draft, Clinton ordered 100 active marksmen drawn from various pre-existing units, including the Loyal American Regiment, King's American Regiment, and DeLancey's Cowboys, to join this new brigade.

Armed with rifles and dressed in green coats with white stripes, the group became known as Emerich's Chasseurs. Among its members were Westchester men Benjamin Ogden, Thomas Merritt, and The Bronx's Major Manfield Bearsmore. The group also had several offshoot groups, including one led by Hessian Johann Althouse.

Known locally as The Sharpshooters, Johann Althouse led his group of several dozen riflemen on an attack on Wright's Mills on January 2, 1778. The event captured the attention of Continental Army Major General Israel Putnam (the future namesake of Putnam County, NY), who wrote to General George Washington about the skirmish.

Putnam noted that after The Sharpshooters surprised the Wright's Mills militia guard, which included Thomas Wright's son William and his father-in-law, blind military veteran Robert Lyon, they quickly fled the scene. A rebel party of 17 boatmen from Tarrytown under Captain Buchanan tracked them fleeing the area, eventually engaging in combat with the riflemen later that night near the border of modern-day Valhalla and White Plains.

The clash happened at the Joseph Young House. Joseph Young had served as a sergeant in the Continental Army, and his stone house and barn became a fortified camp and tavern, for the Patriots. General Putnam told Washington that "the enemy gave way and fought on the retreat for several miles. Our party pursued them, killed and captured the whole, except for two. Our only loss was Captain Buchanan."

Allegedly, Althouse and his son, ensign John Jr., escaped the skirmish by running down "Tucky Hoe Road," where another Loyalist party helped cover them. A year later, the father and son were arrested and sent as prisoners to Long Island. Upon release, they relocated to Canada.

In mid-June of 1778, General Washington and his troops departed from Valley Forge. He instructed Brigadier General Charles Scott to command 1,500 light foot soldiers to harass the British forces as they moved across New Jersey. French Major General Marquis de Lafayette joined Scott with an additional 1,000 men, preparing for a significant attack the following day.

General Charles Lee was George Washington's second-in-command of The Continental Army until his capture in December 1776 by British General Banastre "The Butcher" Tarleton. When seized by Banastre's troops at a tavern in New Jersey, Lee was in the process of writing a letter to Continental Army General Horatio Gates complaining about Washington's deficiency.

The British held Lee captive until a prisoner exchange during the Spring of 1778. Washington greeted Lee enthusiastically when they reunited in Valley Forge. Despite Lee being ignorant of changes during his sixteen months away, Washington put him in charge of a Vanguard and an attack mission

On June 28, 1778, General Lee initiated the attack on British General Henry Clinton's troops near Monmouth, NJ. The attack happened a day late without Lee informing General Washington or Brigadier General Scott of his battle plan.

For one reason or another, there was a lot of confusion on the battlefield. By some accounts, some of the Patriot forces appeared to retreat, causing a domino effect of fleeing soldiers, only later to be realized there was no ordered retreat and front-line soldiers had just run out of ammunition. By other accounts, communication issues between General Lee and others led to mass confusion, including the movements of Lee's subordinate generals without his knowledge.

Although Washington's main force eventually arrived, restored order, and prevented the British advance, Washington blamed his generals for running from the enemy. Some historians say that Charles Scott witnessed Washington berating Charles Lee in a profanity-laden tirade after the clash.

Regardless of who was to blame, Washington suspended Lee from command, and the court-martialed him for the retreat. While awaiting trial that summer, Lee was held captive by the Continental Army inside a barn at Reuben's Wright's mill.

From July 20-27, Wright's Mills became Washington's headquarters. That week, the Continental Army General's communications were all addressed: "Head Quarters, Wright's Mill," including notices to and from Marquis de Lafayette and Alexander Hamilton. Washington even hosted a War Council meeting there, attended by numerous high-ranking officials. He also restocked supplies for the army, including chickens, butter, tea, milk, bread, salt, vinegar, and sugar, for which he received an itemized bill prepared by Reuben Wright.

 While Washington stayed at Wright's Mill, perhaps for added protection from potential marauding Cowboys, Charles Scott was brought in to lead a militia from Stockbridge, Massachusetts, comprised of Native Americans.

 Despite some Native American groups, including the Mohawks of the Iroquois Confederacy, fighting alongside the British, a group of Wappingers aligned with the Patriots. Sachem Daniel Ninham and his son Abraham captained the Stockbridge Militia, who had previously fought alongside the Continental Army at the Battle of Monmouth.

 While stationed in Wright's Mills, the mission of the Stockbridge Militia was to patrol White Plains and parts of nearby Westchester to gather intelligence on British troop movements. On August 20, they ambushed Emerich's Chasseurs, killing one of their riflemen and wounding another. After the skirmish, news about this Native American force spread to British intelligence.

 On August 31, a Continental Army unit and the Stockbridge Militia ambushed a Hessian company in Yonkers. They killed six Hessians, forcing the others to retreat towards New York City—the British plotted retaliation by setting a trap.

Three high-ranking officers were involved in implementing the plan: Chasseurs leader Andreas Emerich, British General Banastre "The Butcher" Tarleton, and Tarleton's close friend John Graves Simcoe.

Simcoe commanded an elite group of about 50 Loyalists known as The Queens Rangers. Simcoe took over the group a year prior, replacing the group's previous leader, Lieutenant Colonel Robert Rogers. Known as "The White Devil," the once-elite Rogers was dismissed for "poor health," however, some believe he had a problem with alcohol.

The three men devised a trap and set it into action on the northern edge of Van Cortlandt Park, near the Bronx's border with Westchester County.

Emerich's Chasseurs drew the Wappinger militia out into the open, and then Simcoe's Rangers struck, hitting the militia's left flank. The vastly outnumbered Native American warriors attempted to fight back in brutal hand-to-hand combat.

Tarleton's light cavalry, the First Dragoon Guards, then entered the battle and broke the Wappingers' line of defense, resulting in many of the Stockbridge Militia being hunted down and killed. According to Simcoe's journal, Daniel Nimham told his warriors that "he was old and would stand and die there." A Dragoon Guard, Private Edward Wight, cut him down and killed him.

By most accounts, roughly 40 Stockbridge Militia were killed in the battle, while the Queen's Rangers suffered comparatively light losses, with one cavalryman killed and three wounded. Due to the chaos of the fight, the Stockbridge Militia did not bury their casualties, though local residents quickly combed over the battlefield and buried any bodies they found. By the 19th century, the spirit of the slain sachem has been said to haunt the land known as "Indian Field".

After leaving Wright's Mills, Washington headquartered in White Plains at the Purdy House, where he had previously stayed in 1776. While there, the surviving members of the Stockbridge Militia requested to return home to help the families of the dead. The survivors were paid $1,000 (approximately $42,000 today) for their service and discharged by Washington.

Meanwhile, Charles Lee's court trial had concluded. The court charged Lee with disobeying orders, not attacking the morning of the battle, conducting an unnecessary, disorderly, and shameful retreat, and disrespecting the commander-in-chief. Lee's defense was articulate but fatally flawed by his efforts to turn it into a personal contest between himself and Washington. The court found Lee guilty on all charges, ending his military career.

During this time, another skirmish took place. Captain Daniel Williams commanded a group of Patriots quartered at The Joseph Young House. Williams led a raid against Loyalist targets during a three-day snowstorm. Accompanied by numerous other Patriots, including Westchester teenage guide Abraham Requa, the Patriot forces captured several Loyalist militia leaders.

On Christmas Eve 1778, Emerich's Chasseurs responded with a raid on Young's House, where they burnt one of the barns, took some cattle, and captured several American prisoners, including Captain Williams, Sgt. Joseph Young, Isaac Van Tassel, and others. Abraham Requa and about twenty others fled to safety in Wright's Mills, where Colonel John Jameson was stationed with a detachment of the Continental Army.

5.) YOUNG AMERICANS

With temperatures dropping below freezing for several weeks and snowfall measured in feet rather than inches, the winter quickly became known as the worst in memory. Shortly after New Year's Day 1780, the Continental Army gained intelligence that several of Delancey's Cowboys were stationed in a house near New Rochelle. Captains Samuel Keeler and Samuel Lockwood led a militia of about 80 men on a night raid of the property.

The raiders attacked the home, shooting three guards and killing a horse belonging to Cowboys' Colonel Isaac Hatfield. Alerted to the attack, about fifteen Cowboys led by Hatfield fired back from an upper story of the house. After nearly 20 minutes, the Patriots threatened to burn the house with the men inside, leading to a surrender.

General William Heath described the incident in his journal:

"The Colonel and his men took to the chambers and fired out at the windows and downstairs at those who had entered the house; it appeared difficult, if possible, to dislodge them; the house was instantly set on fire by putting a straw bed into a closet [i.e., small room], which compelled the enemy to jump out at the chamber windows, to avoid the flames."

The militia captured Hatfield and fourteen others and successfully got all of the prisoners back to American lines except for one. Thomas Huggeford escaped and joined with allies, including James DeLancey, to retaliate.

Heath wrote to Washington:

"Huggeford had indeed collected thirty-four cavalry of his corps, supported by twenty-eight infantry, "continued the pursuit, and came up with their rear between New-Rochelle and Mamaroneck, and resolutely closing with them, killed 23, and took 40 prisoners, some of whom are wounded."

A few weeks later, on February 2, another raging snowstorm hit Westchester. Around 11 pm, a massive unified force of about 500 men comprised of DeLancey's Cowboys, Simcoe's Rangers, Emerich's Chasseurs, The Sharpshooters, and British Army and Hessian regiments launched a surprise attack on nearly 250 American soldiers stationed at The Joseph Young House near the border of White Plains and Valhalla.

After a brief long-range gunfight, the Patriot picket guard surrendered. Soon after, a second skirmish between the Americans and the Loyalist attackers ensued, going back and forth for several minutes until the outnumbered Americans could no longer fend off the enemy. Several Americans were mortally wounded as the attackers took control of the property.

As the attackers seized 76 American prisoners, they set fire to The Joseph Young House and its surrounding buildings. They left the wounded soldiers behind in the apple orchard behind the burning house.

After destroying Young's House, the raiding party targeted the nearby Carpenter House, which sheltered American soldiers recovering from smallpox. British soldiers forced all of the sick men out into the deep snow, causing their deaths. The site of the tragedy later became part of the Westchester Community College campus.

Fortunately, the events that transpired on February 3, 1780, were the last documented Revolutionary War clashes in Westchester County. However, a historic event was about to unfold.

While stationed on Long Island, Queens Rangers leader John Simcoe became fascinated with the homeowner's 18-year-old daughter, Sarah "Sally" Townshend. On February 14, 1780, he declared his feelings for her in a handwritten love poem. However, Sarah declined Simcoe's advances because she wanted to get to know another British soldier at the house visiting Simcoe, the head of British intelligence, Major John Andre.

Despite Simcoe's romantic advances and inadvertently sending the first Valentine's Day card in history, Sally favored the charming Andre. According to legend, one evening, Sarah overheard them discussing plans to capture the American fort West Point thanks to the treachery of American General Benedict Arnold. Sarah transmitted the information to her brother Robert, who, along with Benjamin Tallmadge, were leaders of George Washington's Culper Spy Ring.

After secretly communicating for months by utilizing Benedict Arnold's wife, Peggy Shippen, as a go-between, on September 22, 1780, John Andre and Benedict Arnold met in person.

Andre traveled up the Hudson River on the British gunship *Vulture* and met with Arnold in a wooded area near the shoreline of Rockland County, NY, near the site of the American fort West Point. The pair talked for hours, during which Arnold agreed to accept a payment from the British Army to switch sides during the war and surrender the American fort he commanded to the British Army. Arnold turned over six handwritten papers that showed the British how to take West Point, which Andre hid in his stocking.

During their secret meeting in the Rockland County woods, a Westchester Militia attacked *Vulture*, forcing it to flee and leaving Andre abandoned.

After ferrying across the Hudson, Andre traveled southward from Yorktown. Dressed in civilian clothes, he hid the papers from Arnold in one of his boots as he rode a horse towards the British lines in Manhattan. Early in the morning on September 17, 1780, Andre rode south through Westchester. His route took him from King Street in Chappaqua down to Hardscrabble Road, near the border of what is now Briarcliff Manor and Pleasantville. He rode past the house of Westchester Militia sergeant Sylvanus Brundage and stopped at a small stream in front of house #80 so his horse could drink water.

Andre continued down to Old Bedford Road, passing Abraham Requa's house. His mother spotted the strange horseman on the road and tried alerting her son, who was patrolling nearby with a local militia, but the horseman didn't remain stationary. Andre continued his journey into Tarrytown, where he encountered three men.

Local militiamen David Williams, Isaac Van Wart, and John Paulding were patrolling the Albany Post Road in Tarrytown when Andre rode through. They found him suspicious, stopped him, and asked him some questions.

In perhaps the first case of someone using a fake I.D. in Westchester County history, Andre produced a pass given to him by Arnold that falsely identified him as an American named "John Anderson". The militiamen didn't buy his story and quickly searched him. After discovering the hidden documents in "John Anderson's" boot, Andre tried to bribe the men. They declined the bribe and had him arrested.

In another version of the story, Andre mistook the three militiamen for British allies because John Paulding, who had just escaped from jail, wore a Hessian jacket. Thinking he was amongst friends, Andre identified himself as a British officer and, in turn, was arrested.

The Westchester militiamen took "John Anderson" to a Continental Army base at Wright's Mill. Colonel Jameson, who had served under Benedict Arnold, conducted a thorough interview with suspect. During the interview, Jameson discussed the situation with Benjamin Tallmadge.

The Culper Spy Ring leader had already started piecing together what was happening and urged Jameson to refrain from informing Arnold about their detainee. While "John Anderson" was locked in a Wright's Mill barn, Jameson exposed the situation to Arnold. Due to the severity of everything, Jameson also alerted General Washington.

Washington reviewed the found papers. When Washington called for "Anderson" to be brought to him, the spy finally confessed that he was—in fact—British Major John Andre.

After receiving the news of Andre's capture, Benedict Arnold fled to safety in British-held New York City. He managed to get there undetected by sailing on Vulture. Arnold joined the British army and was part of the forces that captured Charleston, South Carolina.

While Major Andre awaited trial, the once-elite regiment Emerich's Chasseurs suffered a fatal defeat. A Patriot force did not eliminate the group. Instead, they fell victim to a mutiny within their own ranks.

American members generally opposed Emerich's leadership, while the Europeans supported his decision-making. Some officers deserted the group, and Emerich filed disputes against his men, who in turn filed counter-disputes against him. After disbanding, some members joined other units, such as Simcoe's Rangers and DeLancey's Cowboys. Soon after, Andreas Emerich left America for Europe.

That October, Major John Andre was tried as a spy, hanged, and buried in an unmarked grave. While considered a villain in America, the English viewed him as a hero. Years later, Andre's body was exhumed and reburied in London's Westminster Abbey.

In Westchester, there was a growing sense of patriotism that led to the targeting of another formerly elite group. According to local lore, later that fall, several Patriots found a floating body in the Bronx River. Once they identified the corpse as one of their comrades, Westchester militiaman Nicholas Odell plotted revenge against his friend's killers, DeLancey's Cowboys.

Odell, whose ancestor Samuel Odell was the final prisoner seized by the infamous pirate Blackbeard, obtained intelligence that The Cowboys would be passing by the Bronx River later that day in the White Plains area. The Americans ambushed their targets, forcing them to flee over the frozen water. The ice was thin and cracked, causing around fifteen Cowboys to drown in the freezing water. The area in the marshlands above White Plains in The Bronx River became known as Dead Man's Lake.

On July 4 and 5, 1781, General Washington and Rochambeau and their respective armies met at Wright's Mills. This was a favored location for Washington as he felt the terrain provided good protection. Many well-known individuals, such as Alexander Hamilton, Aaron Burr, Israel Putnam, Nathaniel Greene, and Lafayette, had previously met with Washington at this location. This particular meeting may have been when Washington and Rochambeau discussed their plans for the upcoming months.

In the autumn of that year, the Continental Army and their French allies achieved a decisive victory over the British forces at the Battle of Yorktown in Virginia. Despite being outnumbered and outmatched, the American troops managed to sustain a three-week siege, which resulted in significant losses for the British. Eventually, the British were forced to surrender, paving the way for the end of British colonial rule and the birth of the United States of America. The British surrender marked the beginning of peace negotiations and ultimately led to the signing of the Treaty of Paris.

The end of the American Revolution led to a mass departure of Loyalists in January 1782. Nearly 100,000 people who remained loyal to the British Crown left America to find new lives in England, Canada, and British Colonies in the West Indies. Among them were about 15,000 African Americans, some of whom helped to found the country of Sierra Leone in Africa. Other departures included soldiers and members of groups like The Cowboys and The Queens Rangers.

On Thursday, December 4, 1783, nine days after the last British troops left American soil, George Washington gathered with his officers at a New York City tavern to thank them for their service. He bid them an emotional farewell before returning home. Before being faced with brick and used as a tavern, the building was a lower Manhattan townhouse owned by French immigrant Entien DeLancey, the father of "The Outlaw of the Bronx" Oliver DeLancey and great-uncle of Cowboys leader James DeLancey.

After the war, James DeLancey retired to Nova Scotia, Canada. He settled on a 640-acre estate near the Bay of Fundy with his young wife, infant child, and six slaves. He became involved in local politics. His involvement in a debate defending the legality of slavery in Nova Scotia resulted in one of his enslaved workers, Jack, escaping to freedom in the province's capital city, Halifax.

DeLancey even tried to sue the Supreme Court for the payment of wages Jack had earned while working as a free man in Halifax, but before a resolution, he passed away. According to family tradition, DeLancey had promised freedom to one of his female slaves, so she poisoned him.

Years later, in 1821, Westchester author Fennimore Cooper popularized fictional stories of The Cowboys and the Neutral Ground in his novel *The Spy*. Some believe his fictional tale may have been inspired by stories told to him by his wife, Susan DeLancey.

John Simcoe also moved to Canada. He established York, later renamed Toronto, the country's largest city. Simcoe became the first Lieutenant-Governor of Upper Canada, later named Ontario. During his tenure, he introduced institutions such as the trial by jury and passed the first Act Against Slavery in the British Empire. Although Americans often view him negatively, Canadians consider him a heroic founding father and honor him annually with the holiday Simcoe Day.

Sally Townshend never married but kept Simcoe's love poem until she passed away years later. Historians deem it to be the first-ever Valentine's Day card. According to local rumors, Sally's ghost still stalks her old home where she met Simcoe and John Andre, Raynham Hall in Oyster Bay, NY.

As a reward for apprehending Major Andre, Congress awarded Isaac Van Wart a farm in Duchess County, NY. He promptly exchanged the property for land in Westchester, specifically where The Joseph Young House once stood. There, he built a large farmhouse near the former house's foundation.

Today, the house blends in amongst the many additions to the main building of Westchester's Blythedale Children's Hospital. Family tradition maintains that Isaac's house is the central gabled portion, with the great red brick fireplace chimney facing Knollwood Road.

As the war ended and the residents of Wright's Mills celebrated their independence, the small farming village was about to face even more changes.

6.) THIRTEEN TERRIBLE TALES

Over the eighteenth century, Wright's Mills underwent several name changes. Following the passing of Thomas Wright in 1786, his son William sold the family property to William Latting, who in turn sold it to Thomas Sands just a few years later in 1790. The land that Thomas and his wife Rachel acquired included 124 acres combined with its houses, barns, mills, dams, ponds, and streams. A few years later, Thomas resold it to his brother John Sands.

 John was an ambitious businessman who worked as a blacksmith. Amongst the additions he made to his property included the addition of an oil mill and a yarn factory. The house he lived in was built in 1809 and became locally known as The Mansion House.

 When John died in 1832, his property was divided and sold at auction. Various millers came and went, causing the neighborhood's name to change each time. Sands Mills became Robbins Mills and then became Carpenter's Mills. After Mr. Carpenter passed away, the auction for his possessions was still in progress while the village was renamed Knowlton Mills.

 A relative of Mr. Carpenter, Ingersoll Knowlton, bought a lot of the property. The choice to cease the yarn plant resulted in the factory's two-storied wooden buildings and machinery sitting idle for years. buildings and their machinery sat idle for years at Knowlton's Mills.

The Methodist pastors, including the popular John Robbins, preached at the village's old red schoolhouse for many years. By 1835, the meetings were becoming so crowded that Kensico needed a church to accommodate its citizens. Later that year, Kensico's Methodist Church was built, along with ample space for a cemetery.

Service on the Metro North Harlem Line began extending railroad service from New York City into Westchester in multiple stages starting in December 1840. A year later, service extended to Fordham, and in 1842 reached Williams Bridge. By 1844, stations were built in Tuckahoe and White Plains, and in October 1846, the train line ended at the Knowlton Mills community at a station named Davis Brook. A horse-drawn stage transported travelers to and from the train station into town.

In the late 1840s, the valley experienced a flourishing period with various industries such as a grist mill, a cider mill, a felt hat factory, a textile mill, and dye works, all powered by the Bronx River and Bear Gutter Creek. Bear Gutter Creek was well-known as a fishing spot for bass, eels, and bullfrogs. New York City's first railroad ran along the 24-mile-long Bronx River, which runs south to the northern Bronx.

Land values near the train line experienced a significant increase. The shops, hotels, and saloons located near the train station thrived. In contrast to the present times, the primary source of revenue for the Harlem Line railroad was not the passengers but freight. The freight included shoes, hats, paper, flour, carriages, and, most importantly, milk for New York City. The Milk Train enabled local dairy farmers to send their products to New York City, substantially increasing their revenue.

By the mid-1800s, the village's blacksmiths included Benjamin Carpenter, whose shop was next door to his wagon shop, Benjamin Creemer in the central part of the village, and James Edward Stivers' shop just below nearby Armonk's popular Smith's Tavern. The area also had numerous shoemakers, including Hiram Finch, who owned a nearby general store and ran the mail and passenger horse-drawn stagecoach.

As the population expanded, the community established its first post office in 1849 inside the Wykoff family's store. Instead of continuing to name the community after the local mill owner, a local business owner named Jonathan Washington Tompkins suggested the village be named Kensico after Siwanoy leader Sachem Cockensko. The post office and train station also adopted the new name. This name change brought a sense of pride and identity to the growing community.

By the 1850s, a train ride from New York City to Kensico took three hours. Comparatively, an express train from Grand Central Station to North White Plains is about 37 minutes today. Despite the trains moving much slower than we may comprehend today, several horrible disasters happened on the tracks.

On a Saturday afternoon in May 1854, as resident Mrs. Henry Hunter tried exiting the train at the Kensico station, the train started to move. The 65-year-old woman fell and got crushed under a wheel. The train severed both of her legs.

In November 1856, a train near Kensico derailed. The train consisted of a baggage car, eight milk cars, and two passenger cars filled with people. A large piece of fallen wood on the tracks caused the eight milk cars to be violently thrown down an embankment, smashing to pieces and frightening the passengers.

Fortunately, the passenger cars remained on the train, and all passengers survived. Several, however, received injuries, including one man who was thrown entirely over the wires of the telegraph alongside the track and three others who received broken bones and internal injuries. During the chaos, a milk train employee named John Markoe was injured, and the 26-year-old brakeman Daniel Murray was killed.

Among the Milk Train incidents in 1859 was one in August, when, for unknown reasons, Kensico station's track master Alexander Carrigan jumped on one of the cars about a mile from the nearby Mt. Kisco station. About an hour later, pedestrians passing along the track discovered his mangled body. Doctors urgently treated him and fully amputated one of his arms, but a few days later, he died.

As the newly renamed community grew, including the addition of saloons, shops, and hotels, so unfortunately did a number of shocking events. Over the next ten decade or so, an unlucky series of thirteen strange and unfortunate events struck the growing village.

<u>I.) The Secret Agent</u>

 On a spring day in 1868, a sharp-dressed and handsome man boarded a train in White Plains. He had a train ticket for Kensico and struck up a conversation with Mr. Flewellin, the owner of Kensico's flourishing flour mill. During their conversation, he mentioned that he was an agent for a new product that could restore hair loss. He also told Mr. Flewellin he was meeting a friend at Kensico train station to discuss business.

 When the train arrived, the handsome stranger noticed his friend was not there to pick him up. He approached Mr. F and asked for directions to a nearby hotel. However, instead of directing him to a hotel, Mr. F offered to help him find a place to stay. Mr. F suggested they try Mr. Carpenter's nearby residence, but Mr. Carpenter refused to accommodate a random stranger. Fortunately, Justice Wykoff, who lived nearby, was willing to provide a room to the stranger and welcomed him into his home.

 The following day, the handsome stranger informed Justice Wykoff that he was having such a good time at his house that he decided to extend his stay for a few more days. While in Kensico, he attended multiple parties and received attention from several women.

On the fourth day of the handsome agent's stay, Justice Wykoff and his friend Mr. Ferris awakened to a surprise; they had been robbed. The handsome guest who had been staying in the house where the robbery took place was missing, along with $100 cash (worth about $2,300 today) and a gold watch.

II.) The Dog Days of Summer

In Kensico, the summer of '69 was a time of beauty and terror. The warm sun shone down on the rolling fields of wheat and barley, and the sound of cicadas filled the air. But the peace was shattered when a large black Newfoundland passed through the village, biting every animal in its path. Rumors quickly spread that the dog had rabies, and the town was thrown into a state of panic. As more and more dogs fell victim to the disease, the townspeople became increasingly desperate. The quick spread of rabies through the town triggered many of its citizens to grab their guns. Locals caught the Newfoundland and shot it. Every additional dog who was bitten or even suspected of being bitten was rounded up and shot, as the once-idyllic town was consumed by fear and paranoia.

Later that summer, there were reports of a stray dog that had not been muzzled and was seen attacking and biting livestock, including sheep and hogs. The situation escalated when the same dog bit a dog belonging to a local resident named Henry Reynolds. A butcher wagon driver in the vicinity saw the chaos and attempted to run over the wild dog but was unsuccessful. A group of concerned individuals managed to corral the dog in a wagon house, where they ultimately had to shoot it. Unfortunately, as a precautionary measure, the animals bitten by the rabid dog were also killed

As the dog's summer days ended, a fire destroyed a mill belonging to John W. Tompkins, the namer of Kensico village. Used by a New York firm as a factory, the entire structure was engulfed in flames and destroyed within an hour.

<u>III.) The Nude Intruder</u>

While wild dogs spread rabies throughout Kensico during the summer of 1869, another pandemic also began to break out in town: smallpox. Among the infected was the young child of Mr. and Mrs. Hall. On an exceptionally humid July night, the Halls finally got their infant child to sleep around 11 pm. The uncomfortable humidity in the Kensico summer air led the adults to move a couch into the dining room and open several doors to create a cross breeze. Shortly around midnight, however, something strange awoke Mr. Hall.

Aroused by a noise from within the house, Mr. Hall abruptly jumped up from the couch around midnight. Immediately noticing that his once brightly burning kerosene lamp had been turned down and almost extinguished, he called, "Who's there"? He received no reply, but moments later, something caught his eye.

He saw a barefoot man not wearing a shirt and perhaps nothing else lurking in the darkness, hovering over the sick child's crib. As Mr. Hall approached, the strange intruder disappeared through the outer door. Mr. Hall pursued, and as his approach grew closer, he recognized the man and even called out to him by name. Unfortunately, Mr. Hall, a horizontally-gifted gentleman, tripped and fell, leading to the naked intruder's escape into the night's darkness.

Early the following day, Mr. Hall alerted Justice John Wykoff, who, based on Hall's complaint, procured a warrant for the arrest of Dodrigde Daniels, a man who used to work for Mr. Hall. An officer arrested Daniels and brought him in for questioning. Daniels not only denied the allegations but also produced an alibi. Daniels' new employer swore he was home in bed at the time of the burglary and was at work, as usual, in the morning.

Mr. Hall produced two pieces of evidence he found on his property scattered by the front gate the morning after the home invasion: a yarn jacket and a pair of shoes. Despite the physical evidence, Daniels denied owning the items, and the police released him. Public opinion around town, however, was that Daniels was guilty of the break-in, especially as this wasn't his first run-in with the law.

Just a few weeks earlier, police arrested Daniels in Port Chester after beating his wife. A few days after Daniels' release from jail, he got into a screaming match with several members of the Fisher family in Port Chester. Things escalated when Daniels followed one of the men into a saloon on Purchase Street and violently waved a weapon. The police arrested Daniels, but according to reports from the *Port Chester Journal*, Daniels "refused to stay arrested and the constable permitted him to escape, in such an open and uncalled for, and what s claimed cowardly-manner, as to provoke jeers from the large crowd assembled." Days later, the injuries he inflicted on his wife during the violent assault resulted in her death.

<u>IV.) On Thin Ice</u>

On Saturday, December 2, 1871, the Patterson family took a quick trip from New York City to Kensico to visit Caroline's sister, Anne, and her family. The Montforts were well-known in the village because Anne's husband, Albert, operated a popular grocery store on the bottom floor of their three-story house.

After the weekend, Caroline's husband, John, returned to New York City for work. Caroline opted to stay in Kensico for a few more days so her children, ten-year-old George and six-year-old Carrie May, could play with their cousin, Albertina, nicknamed "Bertie."

The next day, the kids eagerly played outside in the winter snow. At one point, they began gliding over the ice of a nearby frozen sawmill pond in a sled. The children didn't return to the house, causing the adults to search for them.

The parents quickly noticed a collapse in the millpond's ice and soon discovered the lifeless bodies of the three children, drowned. Following a funeral in Kensico, the three children were laid to rest in Sleepy Hollow.

V.) Lunacy

In mid-December 1871, a Kensico resident named James Scanlon went on a sudden rampage. He visited his neighbor's residence, Mr. Harris, and for unknown reasons, began smashing his windows and doors. A few local men, including Scanlon's father-in-law, rushed to the scene to subdue him. A struggle ensued; Scanlon bit his father-in-law, and the police got involved After the incident, Scanlon, who had been dubbed "The Lunatic" by local newspapers, became lodged in a cell in the county house.

Perhaps inspired by Scanlon's outburst, a few days later, a group of men who worked on the nearby railroad near Rye Lake got heavily intoxicated at a Kensico hotel. The drunken laborers then began a physical altercation with each other before being broken up and kicked out of the establishment.

<u>VI.) A Narrow Escape</u>

On a Tuesday evening in late February 1872, Mr. and Mrs. Hall rode into town in a two-horse wagon with Mrs. Hall's sister and a driver. As they approached the big hill leading into Kensico, terror struck. The wagon's pole fell to the ground, and the out-of-control wagon ran on the heels of the horses, who quickly became unmanageable, blitzing down the hill, viciously kicking in fear.

The driver and Mr. Hall sprang from the wagon, landing safely. The ladies were less fortunate. Mr. Hall's sister-in-law was thrown over the wheel and violently thrown to the ground, resulting in severe bruising. Mrs. Hall was thrown from the fast-moving wagon and struck the ground with such force that it caused numerous lacerations, a concussion, and blood freely spewing from her ears, mouth, and nose.

After reaching the bottom of the hill, the horses kicked themselves from the wagon. They ran through the village, eventually colliding with the Armonk stagecoach in front of Albert Montfort's grocery store.

VII.) Charred

For the first two weeks of March 1872, scarcely a night passed without a raging fire visible from the summit of Kensico's Big Hill. One Friday night, eight fires broke out within two hours, including one to the east on the allegedly haunted Buckout Road and one on White Plains' Chatterton Hill, which saw action during the Revolutionary War.

All along the line of the Harlem Railroad, fires have left blackened fields and charred vegetation. While some locals lived in fear of potential arson, a group of local religious fanatics instead believed the fires might be a sign of the return of Jesus Christ.

VIII.) Wrong Side of The Tracks

After having a few drinks at a local Kensico establishment, 35-year-old Patrick Donelly began his stumbling walk home. He'd often cut across the train tracks and, in the past, had previously experienced several narrow escapes from instant death from being struck by a train.

Despite the store owner warning Patrick to stay off the tracks, around 8 pm, a speeding express fatally train struck him down. After the train had passed, about 200 yards away, locals found his horribly mangled body.

IX.) The Shotgun Engagement

A romantic encounter transpired during a train ride from New York City to White Plains on a chilly night in 1873. The charming Robert Wilson from White Plains met Kate Lowery from Kensico and instantly hit it off, chatting until they reached their destination. As they stepped off the train, Robert proposed to drive her home to Kensico in a sleigh. Kate agreed, and before they arrived at her father's house, the two had already decided to get married.

Their evening of bliss was cut short because Kate's father, John Lowery, was less than pleased with the sudden engagement. When the sleigh arrived at his gate around 2 am, the enraged father forbade the engagement and threatened to hang Robert with a piece of rope before slamming the door in his face.

A week later, Robert got together with his pals Jas Johnson and "Swearing" Sam Carpenter. The trio, with the help of Kate's sister, devised a plan to abduct the bride-to-be.

Around 8 pm on a chilly January Friday night, the sleigh from White Plains arrived at the Lowery mansion. While the men hid, Kate's sister went into her father's house and asked Kate if she wanted to go for a sleigh ride. Mr. Lowery, not suspecting any conspiracy, raised no objection, and Kate left.

The group made it about four miles in the snow until something startled them. A gunshot rang out, followed by a scream in a familiar voice, "Stop, or I'll shoot again!" Mr. Lowery yelled as he chased them on horseback. The sleigh's horses bucked as another blast from Mr. Lowery's shotgun fired. After about a half-dozen shots, the sleigh came to a halt.

The driver, "Swearing Sam," leaped out of the vehicle, swiftly trampled through the snow, and lunged up a nearby apple tree to evade the shotgun-wielding old man. With his gun pointed at the men, Mr. Lowery demanded the sleigh turn around and return to Kensico. "Don't shoot Mr. Lowery! I'll come down!" Sam sacredly screamed. "The marriage shall not take place; just drive back!" Mr. Lowery ordered.

Sam grabbed the reins while Johnson cracked the whip, and the sleigh quickly took off. However, as they fled from Kensico, an angry father on the road started shooting at them. Even though Mr. Lowery pursued them on horseback, the sleigh lost him around 1 am in Tarrytown.

After seeing how distressed her father was, Kate's sister changed her mind about supporting the marriage. The next night, as the sleigh headed towards White Plains, she boarded the express train. The train arrived at White Plains station just as the sleighing party was nearing the Orawampum Hotel.

Outside the hotel, the sisters engaged in a war of words. Kate was warned her father was on the way with two shotguns and three pistols, swearing he would shoot the whole eloping party. Kate and Robert slipped away in the sleigh before an irate Mr. Lowery arrived on the scene waving his artillery. Robert and Kate's sleigh went to the residence of Reverend Van Kleek at Grace Church, who married them that night.

X.) Catch the Stampede

In 1864, stagecoach millionaire Ben "Doc" Holladay came to town and purchased a gigantic amount of property bordering Buckout Road on the outskirts of Kensico in Purchase, NY. Not to be confused with Wyatt Earp's gun slinging pal with a similar-sounding name, this Doc was a business tycoon millionaire. To be clear, he had millions of dollars in the mid-1800s, worth an unimaginable amount today.

On the 100 acres in Purchase Doc bought from David Havilland of the Havilland China family, he built his new wife Anne a magnificent six-story, 84-room mansion. The dining room was large enough to seat 150 guests, which made sense for Doc as he had many high-caliber friends, including Buffalo Bill Cody, Brigham Young, Snowshoe Thompson, Wild Bill Hickok, Ulysses S. Grant, and Abraham Lincoln. The estate, Ophir Farm, was named after a silver mine Doc won in a poker game.

Amongst Doc's hobbies was landscaping. He developed Ophir Farm to capture the flavor of the Wild West with various wildflowers and trees. He stocked the property's streams with speckled trout and purchased numerous animals for the grounds, including horses, deer, antelope, and elk. He was rightfully proud of his estate and enjoyed conducting tours on board a narrow-gauge railroad running around the property.

Doc kept adding more and more to his estate, including a stone church, complete with its own minister to conduct private mass for the family. Perhaps his final and largest addition was the buffalo park.

Doc brought in numerous buffalo from Wyoming. These were the first buffalo on the East Coast, and early maps marked a large portion of the grand estate as "Buffalo Park." Doc hosted buffalo hunts on his property for guests. While it's unclear if any of Doc's famous pals partook in the shooting festivities, in the Spring of 1874, the seven buffalo escaped.

The behemoth animals quickly became a nuisance for neighboring farmers as the wild herd ate everything in sight and caused chaos and destruction in their path. In early January 1875, large prints in the snow led a group of buffalo hunters to Kensico. Eventually cornered in a wooded area, hunters took down the largest male. He weighed a monstrous 1,000 pounds. The fallen buffalo's mate made a desperate charge at the hunters, but they shot her. For the people in Kensico, this was the first time many had seen a bison, dead or alive.

Years later, part of Doc's Ophir Farm property was acquired by Manhattanville College for their campus. Years later, Nestle, the world's largest food and beverage company, purchased another portion of Ophir Farm for its headquarters site.

XI.) Freedom Vision

On July 1, 1876, as the nation prepared to celebrate the 100th anniversary of its freedom from British rule, a hard-working Irish immigrant, Joseph Egan, repaired a wagon inside a Kensico barn belonging to his employer, the Chauncey Smith. Chauncey's son,

Chauncey Smith Jr., was also busy celebrating that day, playing with his new pistol. The 14-year-old startled Egan by playfully shouting, "Your money or your life!" followed by pretending to fire the gun.

Unfortunately, the gun fired a bullet, which struck Joseph in the face, eventually causing him to lose one of his eyes. Ultimately, the case went to court. Joseph sought $10,000 in damages, while the Smith family claimed the incident was purely an accident. The judge awarded Joseph $1,500 for his lost eye.

XII.) The House Guest From Hell-ingone!

In the summer of 1877, Kensico village residents were stunned by the sudden appearance of foul-smelling old rags, dilapidated hats, boots, and feathers scattered throughout the community. Fortunately, the mystery was solved rather quickly. The culprit was a robust northeast-by-east wind and lots of stale rainwater. Unfortunately, there was a tougher mystery to solve.

Later that summer, Leonard Farrington was stunned by the sudden appearance of a strange man knocking on the door of his Kensico home. The stranger said he had faced some hardships and was searching for work. As this was 1877 in a small village, Mr. Farrington invited the man inside, made him supper, and gave him a room to sleep in.

That night, Mr. Farrington lay restless in bed, replaying the stranger's words. Aroused by suspicions, he crept slowly from his bed and grabbed his musket. He then rigged his bed to make it appear like he was still under the covers and silently waited for developments.

Around midnight, Mr. Farrington heard three distinct taps outside of the house. Instantly recognizing something was off, the musket-wielding homeowner charged into the guest room. "Quit the house or be blown to Hellingone!" he shouted at his house guest, who quickly ran out of the house.

Mr. Farrington pursued the blitzing stranger and discovered a second man with a horse and a wagon, assumed to be the strange house guest's accomplice in the attempted robbery or perhaps worse.

XIII.) The Millers and Robbins

In late October 1878, a few years after his brother Edward committed suicide by hanging himself, 55-year-old Tunis Miller of Kensico took his life in the same fashion.

Sadly, Mrs. Mary Robbins, the wife of respected Kensico farmer Charles Robbins, ended her life in 1880 by digesting Paris Green as she battled depression caused by the death of her favorite son three years prior.

7.) RAIN DOGS

Despite a small population of around 200 people by 1880, the farming village of Kensico, without electricity or running water, was plentiful in alcohol. The small community had numerous hotels, saloons, a billiards hall, and no establishment requirement to have a liquor license to sell the people's alcoholic beverage of choice, cider.

Cider could be easily obtained in town, and regular drinkers found it far superior to the best whisky. While it was good for business, the abundance of intoxication created concerns about public safety.

In one instance, three visibly intoxicated tramps, claiming to have just been released that morning from the county jail, showed up in town and tried to enter several homes forcibly. After Kensico resident Robert Robbins aimed his double-barreled shotgun through a window at the perpetrators, the drunken trespassers left town.

In another instance, a group of drunken burglars broke into the home of Thomas Parks. Afterward, they attempted to raid Thomas' neighbor John Sherwood's house, but they were greeted by John's son firing a revolver through an open window at the prowlers. The next morning, Mrs. Sherwood had to clean blood stains under the window.

While fighting occurred frequently at local drinking establishments, perhaps the most dangerous situation occurred hours after the saloons closed. After having a few too many, inebriated pedestrians sometimes took shelter at nearby barns until they sobered up enough to journey home. One late Friday night, several drunken farmhands who were incapable of extended pedestrianism crawled into a barn belonging to Dr. Joshua Fowler.

During the cold night, one of the men, John Thompson, woke up because his pants were literally on fire. It's unclear whether the adult playing with matches had been trying to light a fire or had trouble smoking his pipe. Either way, the relatively old barn went up in flames, killing a horse, two pigs, and another man who was sleeping off his boozy night. The fire destroyed all of the barn's contents, including Dr. Fowler's hay and corn stalks. During the commotion, Mr. Thompson and his burned pants stumbled off into the Kensico night.

In response to these incidents, several of Kensico's most respectable young men announced their pledge not to frequent establishments that sold alcoholic beverages. This early local straight-edge movement led to the local billiards hall changing owners and becoming liquor-free.

8.) BREAK ON THROUGH

In 1805, Westchester County resident Hachaliah Bailey made history by importing an elephant to the United States. Initially, he bought the elephant, named Old Bet, to help him with the farm work. However, he soon realized that people found exotic animals fascinating. He started charging 25 cents for people to view the 7-foot-tall farm helper, who was the second elephant in the US at that time. This offbeat business grew quickly, and Bailey eventually became the first American sole owner of a circus. His contribution to the world of entertainment will always be remembered and inspired many others.

After seeing Bailey's booming success in showcasing exotic animals, several of his neighbors tried to replicate his methods, including descendants of Reuben and Thomas Wright. Instead of operating mills like their ancestors, the Wright brothers of Somers operated a menagerie. Their collection included llamas, camels, and pumas, but their main attraction was lions. In 1829, Daniel Wright became the first man to enter a lion's den during a performance in the United States.

Around 1860, Hachaliah Bailey's nephew, Colonel Frederic Harrison Bailey, adopted an orphan named James McGinnis. Eventually, James became the Colonel's assistant and adopted the last name Bailey.

James Bailey followed in Hachaliah's footsteps and, at 22 years old, formed a circus with his friend James Cooper. 1880, Bailey joined forces with the enigmatic visionary P.T. Barnum to create the Barnum

& Bailey Circus.

After several performances at Madison Square Garden, the Barnum & Bailey Circus traveled to Bridgeport, Ct. Somewhere along the way, allegedly, a large panther escaped. A few weeks later, *The Yonkers Gazette* reported, "A large panther escaped from a Connecticut menagerie is said to be roaming the Yonkers woods." A few days later, *The Katonah Recorder* reported, "A panther making havoc in the farm yards of North Castle is said to have escaped from a menagerie while exhibiting in Connecticut."

Over the next few weeks, panther sightings increased, and groups of hunters gathered to track the wild beast. In late June, a party of six expert hunters led by Oscar Purdy and a team of a dozen hounds followed the escaped animal's scent to the Wampus Swamp on the outskirts of Kensico. After an hour of maneuvering through the thick, stubby undergrowth, the team found their target under a huge Tamarack tree.

The men cautiously advanced, but the panther darted up the tree in a flash. Four of the hunters rushed toward the tree, but in an instant, the panther pounced to the ground, striking one of the hunters with its sharp, savage claws, tearing his clothes and lacerating the flesh on his left shoulder blade, stripping his clothing clean. He now bears three deep cuts from the panther's claws from his hips to the knee of his left leg.

In the chaos, the dogs attacked the enraged cat, who shook several of them roughly and then leaped over their heads and vanished from view.

Three of the hunters with a half dozen dogs followed the panther's trail, which led to the mouth of a vast cave in a mountain just southeast of Pleasantville, where the dogs and hunters refused to follow.

The New York Times reported:
"Panther escaped from a circus in Connecticut, which is now ravaging the northern part of Westchester County, in the neighborhood of Rye Pond, near the Village of Kensico."

Numerous witnesses, ranging from children to doctors, have seen the animal. Several farmers have reported the loss of sheep and calves. There were even reports that a boy fishing at St. Mary's Lake (now Silver Lake) near Buckout Road had been attacked and injured by the savage animal.

The horrible news has brought back flashbacks to locals who had to deal with several wildcats, possibly bobcats, in the thick woodland neighborhood of Rye Pond only a few years ago. With the sightings of a large panther, parents have kept their children home from school, unwilling to let them walk on the lonely roads while a predator cat is on the loose.

By the summer, residents of Kensico reported the wild cat had wreaked havoc in their community, and many of its residents grew fearful of going outside after dark in fear of a face-to-face encounter with the panther. As sightings increased, so did the number of hunters in pursuit, at times as many as 70 hunters working together to track the animal.

By late August, reports of a panther sighting 75 miles away in Port Jervis, NY, emerged, though it remains unconfirmed if it was indeed the former circus performer.

9.) SIN

During the start of the 1880s, a scandalous headline dominated the talk of Kensico: police arrested the local Reverend—the dark-haired 40-year-old Reverend John H. Lane. The married father of two children served as Kensico Methodist Church's Reverend for two years. However, his questionable actions over the past 18 months were brought to light by numerous accusers.

The Wykoff family weren't churchgoers, but they operated a general store in town and enjoyed interacting with members of their community. The family invited Reverend Lane to have dinner with them one night. A few days later, he came by their house unannounced. Mrs. Wykoff alleged that Rev Lane kissed her and put his arms around her against her will. She says he came back a day later and apologized for his actions.

Another married Kensico woman, Mrs. Edwin Cox, charged the Rev. with similar accusations. She lives next to the church. Rev Lane had gotten some of her family to help him put up a stovepipe at the church. While they were doing so, he isolated her and said, "Now I have got them all at work, and I have for a kiss." Mrs. Cox says he then put his arms around her and hugged and kissed her despite her resistance.

A third local girl, Carrie Washburn, also came forward. She reported that once, while she was at the well, getting some water, the Rev. appeared, put his arms around her, and kissed her. At the time, Carrie, the daughter of a local farmer, was 15 years old.

The Rev. denied all the allegations. However, the story was quickly picked up in newspapers all over the world from California to Australia. The public became fascinated with the candid kisser, who inadvertently turned into a bit of a celebrity.

Rev Lane's wife, a young and attractive woman, admitted her husband was in the habit of kissing other women, but she saw nothing wrong with his actions. *The New York Times* covered the trial and reported they felt the church believed to be his favor.

At trial, Rev Lane admitted to kissing the two married women, but in what he claimed was an innocent and lawful way. He strenuously denied the alleged criminal misconduct and said he had been the victim of the slander and gossip of a neighborhood that contains nearly 20 couples who have violated their marriage vows and whose chief business is to stir up drama.

After three hours of deliberation, the committee reached a verdict, determining that although the allegations were reprehensible, the accusers failed to prove Rev Lane's guilt in committing immoral conduct. Consequently, he was acquitted and resumed preaching the Gospel, earning an annual salary of $600 (about $45,000 today).

10.) DAMMED

Kensico residents John and Caroline Raven came to town in the 1870s, shortly after immigrating from Germany. The couple settled in the valley, purchased a farm along the river, and converted the main house into a small hotel. The Raven Hotel grew popular with guests, but in 1880, unexpected news impacted their future plans.

Engineers from New York City announced that they were planning to construct an earthen dam in Kensico to create the first small reservoir to store the reserve supply for the city. Waters from the Byram and Bronx Rivers and Big and Little Rye Lake would become available for city purposes.

The engineers' plans included the construction of a forty-five-foot-high dam across the Byram River and a smaller eighteen-foot-tall dam at the outlet of Little Rye Lake, resulting in one massive storage reservoir containing 1,600,000 gallons of water. The concept would provide New York City with 18,000,000 more gallons of water daily. Unfortunately for some Kensico residents, like the Ravens, the proposed location of this gigantic 300-acre reservoir was on their property.

New York City planned to purchase the needed property from Kensico residents for the project. The reactions from the affected parties varied from agreeable to refusal. The industrious Ravens pivoted and did something unexpected. With teams of horses and oxen and dozens of men straining at ropes, the little hotel was rolled up the hill on logs to a point safe from the city's clutches.

Some property owners instead chose to sell their property to New York City but wanted high prices, sometimes demanding $500 per acre for farmland the city valued at $40. The executor of a 61-acre estate belonging to the Hatfield family rejected an offer of $16,000. The Superintendent of Public Works in charge of the project, Mr. Birdsall, often compromised and offered an inflated $250 per acre to acquire the needed land.

Numerous companies bid for the work of constructing the reservoir. In August 1880, E. Mayn Fowler of Watertown was awarded the two-year project for an undisclosed amount, somewhere between $500,000 and $600,000. Work began in September with a small crew of only fifteen men and a goal of clearing the land and building roads for more extensive work in the spring.

As weeks passed, the work crew's size enlarged to about 40. The work crew, however, hit their first snag in December when a bunch of them took their weekly pay and spent it all the following night, getting drunk in White Plains.

The partying laborers drank until the early morning hours, often buying drinks for various White Plains street toughs that joined their bar crawl across the city. The group engaged in several physical brawls along Railroad Avenue before trying to enter a closed bank and assaulting a Black man working at Charlie Hatfield's saloon on Orawanpum Street. At one point, part of the group attempted to rob one of their coworkers, who ran to the doorstep of Reverend Van Keek at

Grace Church for help. The commotion and chaos resulted in the police arresting several of the intoxicated men from White Plains as the Kensico gang returned to the village.

Gangs of reservoir workmen continued to regularly frequent the White Plains pubs, often resulting in noisy demonstrations and violent saloon fights. The people of White Plains responded with loud complaints about the disorderly visitors.

The dam's work crew increased to about 400 by the following summer. Around this time, the violent "sport" of cock fighting became popular in the village. That November, a northbound milk train fatally struck a 27-year-old reservoir worker on the tracks near Kensico Station.

As dam work continued behind schedule, life in the village suddenly paused at the occurrence of perhaps the community's most shocking event to date.

11.) MURDER OF A SALESMAN

A cold case refers to a crime or a suspected crime that remains unsolved and is not currently under investigation. However, new information could potentially lead to its resolution, such as new witness testimony, re-examined archives, new or retained material evidence, or fresh activities of a suspect. In Westchester County, the oldest cold case dates back to an unsolved Kensico murder in 1882.

In addition to the absence of DNA evidence, several news reports about the case contain inconsistent and incorrect information. Fundamental details such as the names, ages, and occupations of the individuals involved vary from one publication to another, leading to a more significant concern about the accuracy of other information.

With the aid of modern technology, such as easy access to historical U.S. Census and marriage records, correcting basic fundamental information has become relatively effortless. However, it may remain difficult to solve the 142-year-old crime and attain justice for the victim of the unsolved Kensico murder.

U.S. Census records show that Albert Montfort was born in 1829. In 1870, he and his wife, Annie Brundage Montfort, resided in Kensico with their young daughter Albertina, nicknamed Bertie. Albert worked as a salesman, operating a store out of the bottom floor of the family's three-story Kensico house.

The house was on a secluded side street, surrounded by thick woods on three sides and near an old inactive sawmill. Its main entrance faced the road, where customers would enter to purchase groceries and various dry goods, ranging from bread to horse collars, that Albert had for sale. The first floor featured a small back room, used as a kitchen and storage for oils, soap, and vegetables, with a door that led outside. The second floor was divided into four rooms: a kitchen, a dining room, a storage room, and an unoccupied spare room. The top floor had a finished bedroom, an unfinished bedroom, and part of an attic.

In 1871, the couple, who were only a year apart in age, experienced an unimaginable tragedy. Six-year-old Bertie drowned in a sawmill pond near the family's house while sledding with her young cousins George and Carrie May Patterson, who also lost their lives on that cold Kensico day. According to local newspapers, Albert fell ill after burying his daughter, but he eventually recovered.

For unknown reasons, in 1879, Albert and Anne separated. On September 2nd that year, 50-year-old Albert remarried Emma Jean Reynolds, an attractive 19-year-old. She gave birth to a son named Clarence that same year, meaning she was pregnant at the time of their wedding.

Immediately, questions come to mind: did Albert cheat on his wife Ann with Emma, resulting in a surprise pregnancy and rushed marriage? Is it possible Emma was pregnant with someone else's child? Or, did things not work out between Albert and Annie, and Albert found his true love with Emma? There are a lot of different possible angles, and while we'll never know for sure, we do know that as of the end of 1879, Albert and Emma lived together in Kensico with a newborn son. According to the 1880 US Census, a three-year-old, Deborah Banker, also resided with them. While Albert operated the store, Emma stayed home with Clarence. She made clothes that Albert sold to locals who frequented the store.

Throughout Kensico, villagers gossiped about the couple, saying the newlyweds constantly quarreled. Neighbors said Emma thought Albert still secretly talked to his ex-wife Annie.

While Emma's accusations may have been baseless, the fighting often escalated, sometimes resulting in Albert kicking Emma out of the house. Despite the constant drama, Emma said the couple would readily make up despite the consistent quarrels.

Emma's father, William Reynolds, passed away when she was young. She was the youngest of her siblings, who all lived in Westchester. Her sister, Mary Reynolds Banker, lived in Tarrytown, her eldest sister, Sarah, lived in North Castle with her husband, and her brother, Charlie Reynolds, worked as a laborer in Yonkers and lived in Kensico with Emma's mom and second husband, farmer Wesley Stilson.

It's unclear if Emma and Albert's ex-wife Anne knew each other. But, there is a possibility the two women not only knew each other but were also related. Emma's sister, Sarah, married a man named David Brundage. Emma's mother, Elizabeth's maiden name was also Brundage. While Brundage may have been a common name in Westchester during the mid-1800s, it's also possible that Emma's husband's ex-wife, Anne Brundage, was related to her either through her mom's side of the family or via her brother-in-law David.

If Albert's ex-wife was related to Emma, it may have contributed to why Emma forbade him from having contact with her. One possible scenario is that Emma was unaware that Albert's ex-wife was her relative until after they married, which may have shocked and enraged her.

While we don't know whether or not Emma had good reason for disliking Anne or suspecting Albert still talked to her, we do know that she was a constant topic of the couple's arguments. In early August 1882, Emma and her sister Sarah attended a friend's funeral. Sarah asked her younger sister how things were going with her marriage and was stunned by Emma's response: "If I find out he's still in touch with his ex-wife, I will cut his throat from ear to ear!"

In the summer of 1882, Emma's sister Mary separated from her husband and started living in Tarrytown with a new partner, Edgar Haight. On August 31, 1882, the couple visited the Montforts in Kensico. The next day, they left for Tarrytown with Emma and her son, planning to attend a church picnic there over the weekend.

On Saturday, September 2, while Albert remained home, tending his store, Emma's brother Charlie visited her and Mary in Tarrytown between 7 and 8 am before the church picnic.

Charlie had some previous problems with the law and served some time in a Westchester jail. Charlie told his sisters he planned to go to New York City later that day and wanted to board a train at a station where he wouldn't be recognized because he had stolen some tools from a man who owed him money and was afraid of being arrested. His sisters noticed he had a five-chambered revolver with him when he left.

Charlie didn't go to New York City as planned. The Chief of Police who had followed him to Tarrytown tracked him to Kensico. He went to Albert's store and stayed there until around midnight.

The following Sunday, September 3, Charlie went back to Tarrytown to visit his sisters. He told Emma that her husband had received payment for a dress she made that he sold at the store. Charlie brought some shirts for his sisters to wash for him and showed them some money he had. He went on to ask Emma where her husband kept his money and where he kept his knife and his gun. Emma replied, "Sometimes in his pocket and sometimes under his pillow."

Emma remembers Charlie staying at Mary's house until Sunday afternoon, around 5:15 pm, then departing, saying he was going to New York City and would return when he had $100. When he left, the sisters joked that they probably wouldn't see him for a while if that were the case.

Despite again saying he was going to New York City, a woman named Lizzie Wiseman reported seeing Charlie later that day at Albert's store in Kensico.

Robert Wilson's wife stopped by the store between 8 and 9 pm that Sunday night, September 3, to buy bread, but Albert was out of stock. As Albert offered her some crackers instead, she noticed "a young man with a florid complexion in the store. It appeared they were having a dispute." Later that night, some locals returning home from a church gathering passed Albert's store. They recall that around 9:40 pm, they saw a light inside the house carried from the store to the rooms upstairs.

Albert's store was typically closed on Mondays, so it seemed normal when it remained closed on Monday, September 4. Albert had previously told some friends he planned to use his day off to take a quick trip to New York City to purchase supplies.

A few Kensico residents recall seeing Charlie near the store that morning. Charlie's stepfather, Wesley Stilson, also walked a half mile from his house to Albert's store that morning to purchase a shirt collar. He later said he was surprised to find the door locked. Mr. Stilson said he also tried knocking on the back door, but nobody answered.

Around 7 pm that Monday night, baker George Mead stopped by Albert's store. Mr. Mead owned a popular bakery on Railroad Avenue and routinely delivered bread to Albert's store. Mr. Mead knocked on the front door, didn't receive a response, and walked around the back as Albert had previously instructed him to do when making deliveries.

The baker walked partly around the house and tapped on the window of the rear room. He heard the savage barking of a dog and the sight of blood splattered on the window panes. Shocked by what he saw, he rushed into the village for help.

Mr. Mead ran up the hill to Squire Archer's store, where some of Albert's friends were hanging out. George Acklery, Samuel Cunningham, and Daniel Wykoff hurried to Albert's store to investigate.

Upon arrival between 7:30 and 8 pm, the men went to the rear of the house, where they found a window and door covered with blood on the outside. Daniel held a lantern against the window and noticed the store's money drawer was half out. The men then pushed in the rear door and discovered Albert lying dead on the kitchen floor in a pool of blood.

His pockets turned inside-out. His head rested on his right arm, his left arm thrown loosely over his body. Someone had attacked him in such a violent way, nearly severing his head from his body.

Albert's body had more gashes on his back, one across the forehead, penetrating the brain and another slicing his skull. The ax used by the murderer made several false blows throughout the room. One crash of the ax had left a deep gash in the boards of the floor, and a similar strike had chipped a piece out of the inside of the door, showing the door must have been open when the murder was committed.

All around the room, on the walls, carpet, stove, curtains, and table, were innumerable spots of blood showing that a hard struggle had taken place. There was so much blood that it seeped into the floor boards and down into the cellar.

Albert's eyeglasses hung from his neck, and a lead pencil lay on the blood-soaked floor near his hand. All of Albert's money was missing. The horrified friends remarked that any of the four ax wounds inflicted were significant enough on their own to cause instant death. They could not readily locate the murder weapon and went to alert the police.

 Coroner Frank Schirmer of White Plains arrived at the scene of the tragedy and arranged a team of men to assist with solving the case. News of the gruesome murder quickly spread, and horrified neighbors rapidly assembled at the house. While Frank obtained the facts, a group of three White Plains undertakers, Messers, Pierre Storm, and William Purdy, placed Albert's body on ice to avoid decomposition.

 Tuesday, September 5, 1882, marked the nation's first Labor Day holiday. While New Yorkers celebrated, Coroner Schirmer continued his murder investigation. Dr. Schmidt and Dr. Curtiss made a post-mortem examination. After reviewing the injuries, including an eight-inch gash splitting Albert's head open, several deep cuts, and a head injury caused by the blunt end of the murder weapon, they determined any of the blows would have proved fatal.

 Schirmer and District Attorney Baker interviewed witnesses and conducted a search party for the murder weapon. Wesley Stilson helped the investigators try to locate the ax. He led investigators in one direction, remarking to the effect that "only a fool would throw the murder weapon into bushes near the crime."

 Shortly after, another man who lived in the neighborhood, Richard Robbins, found the bloody ax near the crime scene in a thick clump of bushes. Robbins was friends with Albert, and according to the 1860 U.S. Census, when he was 14 years old, he lived with Annie Brundage, though it's unclear what their relationship was. The ax had bloodstains, and Albert's gray hair was still attached.

Neighbor Leonard Farrington claimed ownership of the ax and said someone stole it from his woodpile on Sunday afternoon. His home is about 200 feet from the murder scene and is in between Albert's store and the Stilson/Reynolds residence. Mr. Farrington is the same man who, a few years prior, experienced a spooky incident resulting in him chasing two potential criminals off his property with a bayonet.

During the investigation conducted by Coroner Schirmer, he discovered that Albert kept his clothes in a trunk located in the attic of the Montforts' house. However, no women's clothing was found in the couple's home, which seemed odd as it appeared that Emma did not reside there. Schirmer found this unusual, and he sent the police to Tarrytown to notify Emma about the murder and to escort her to Kensico. As the investigation progressed, Schirmer's suspicions began to focus on Charlie and his father-in-law, Wesley Stilson.

Authorities tried to locate Charlie. While searching his house, they found one of his father-in-law's shirts had blood spots on the cuff. The blood raised suspicions enough to arrest Wesley Stilson, but as soon as he offered an explanation about the blood stains, they released him.

Later, near the barn of the Stilson farm, by a bridge over the Bear Gutter Creek, investigators found a man's calico shirt soaked in blood. The shirt appeared like the ones Charlie Reynolds wore. Coroner Schirmer ordered Charlie's arrest and put the Reynolds family under surveillance in connection to the murder of Albert Montfort.

On Wednesday, September 5, Albert was buried in Sleepy Hollow. Emma attended the funeral with her mother, sister Mary, Edgar Haight, and Albert's brother and sister, John Montfort of Fishkill and Mary Montfort Lester. The Westchester County Board of Supervisors offered a $1,000 reward for evidence that would lead to the conviction of Albert's murderer(s).

Later that day, Chief of Police Alfred Lawrence tracked Charlie to Bridgeport, CT. He found him working in a brickyard and discovered stolen furniture and tools in a room he had just rented. Lawrence described Charlie as small, quiet, and timid. His pockets had blood-stained papers and cigars like the ones sold in Albert's store. Chief Lawrence arrested Charlie and held him in the Westchester County Jail in White Plains, awaiting trial for stolen furniture, stolen tools, and murder.

At trial, Charlie admitted to quarrels with Albert but said they were on good terms. He denied having anything to do with Albert's murder and gave a detailed list of his whereabouts over the past few days. The only thing connecting the blood-stained shirt, which when found appeared to be freshly washed, is that it's the same size and has the same collar band as the ones Charlie wears.

Despite Charlie's rebuttals, District Attorney Nelson Baker's inquest led to further suspicion. Charlie's old employer from the Bloomer Brothers & Co shirt factory in Yonkers testified that Charlie had once disappeared with stolen company funds. Investigators next produced a piece of physical evidence found at the murder scene: a torn piece of a man's shirt. Upon further investigation, they determined its owner purchased it from Bloomer Brothers & Co. in Yonkers. Further probing determined the garment was made by a worker named Fannie Fowler, the same woman who recently left her husband, blacksmith Lewis Fowler, to romantically run away with Charlie Reynolds.

The next piece of evidence introduced by the prosecution was a trunk that Chief Lawrence found in the room Charlie had rented in Bridgeport. The police chief showed the trunk's contents, including numerous letters. The correspondence between Charlie and his sister Mary showed they had planned to get Emma out of the house on the weekend of the murder. The family countered by saying that Mary had written a letter to her sister and invited her to a church gathering.

While the police had enough to convict Charlie for the crime of grand larceny for the stolen tools and furniture, they didn't have enough to charge him with murdering Albert Montfort. Wesley Stilson and the Reynolds family all denied having any reason to want to harm Albert and denied any involvement in the crime.

In November 1882, Charlie Reynolds appeared in court in White Plains. To the surprise of the D.A., he admitted to stealing tools from a man in Tarrytown and furniture from a man in Port Chester. In February 1883, the court sentenced Charlie to five years imprisonment for the burglary and three years for the grand larceny.

Meanwhile, Albert's first wife, Anne Brundage, challenged Emma for ownership of Albert's property. Anne notified the White Plains court that she was Albert's only lawful wife and should be entitled to his property, including the house where they lived together in Kensico.

 A year later, the court awarded Albert's property to his second wife, Emma, who had already remarried. Albert's former wife, now known as Emma Lenihan, promptly sold the house where the murder occurred for $400.

While Charlie served his prison sentence at Sing Sing, Coroner Schirmer publicly vowed to convict Wesley Stilson for the murder of Albert's Montfort. Stilson, whom the community shunned, countered by filing a several thousand dollar lawsuit against Schirmer for slander. The court eventually threw out the case.

 On November 17, 1885, Wesley Stilson was found dead at his Kensico home. Initial reports suspected he died of heart disease. The New York-based *The World* newspaper reported that Stilson's death came as District Attorney Baker was about to present the Montfort murder case to the grand jury. "Death has now put an end to further proceedings," the newspaper said, "but there is a suspicion that Stilson's death was not due to natural causes."

12.) WHODUNNIT

The murder of Albert Montfort remains unsolved. While suspicions may have pointed at Charlie Reynolds, he was never found guilty of the crime. After serving his time for stealing furniture and tools, Charlie left New York and started a new life. It remains unknown whether or not he committed the heinous murder, but if he didn't, the question becomes, who did?

Is it possible the killer was someone else connected to Albert? Was Charlie framed? Was the crime something random, like a robbery gone wrong? Many questions remain surrounding Albert Montfort's shocking death.

Described as at times eccentric, Albert studied law, worked as a teacher, operated a store, and belonged to the local Masonic lodge. It remains unclear why anyone would want to harm the man that neighbors all agreed was a well-respected member of the community.

The murder occurred during the construction of the earthen Kensico Dam. Unfortunately, several tragedies happened at the reservoir construction site, including when a derrick fell on worker Peter Foy on October 21, 1882, crushing him to death. The piece of large and heavy machinery also injured two others. Is it at all possible that with an influx of laborers working at the dam, the murder was a robbery gone wrong, committed by a dam worker?

It's perhaps odd that Mrs. Robert Wilson told authorities that when she went to Albert's store to purchase bread on the possible night of the murder, she saw a man quarreling with Albert in the store. It remains unclear who this man was. Had it been Charlie Reynolds, Wesley Stilson, or someone else from the neighborhood, she likely would have referred to them by name instead of "a man." As the murder occurred either that night or early the next morning, the identity of this man may be a crucial piece of evidence.

Shortly before the murder, Emma's sister Mary left her husband, Mr. Banker. It's unclear why The 1880 U.S. Census shows that three-year-old Deborah Banker resided with Emma and Albert Montfort. Is it possible that Mr. Banker had animosity toward the man his daughter lived with?

After leaving her husband, Mary became involved with Edgar Haight. Around the same time, her brother Charlie became romantically involved with Fannie Fowler. Well, that was her name at the time. Her birth name was Fannie Haight, Edgar's sister.

In 1882, Fannie abandoned her husband, Lewis Fowler, a wealthy blacksmith from Greenburgh, NY, and ran off with Charlie Reynolds, taking her baby son. Unfortunately, Fannie died unexpectedly soon after.

Following Fannie's death, her parents, Arden and Minerva Haight, took responsibility for her child. By 1884, Lewis Fowler had remarried and started legal proceedings to regain custody of his now 3-year-old son.

Around noon on Tuesday, June 3, 1884, Lewis saw his son with his grandmother at the Tarrytown train station. A commotion ensued between Lewis and his ex-mother-in-law, resulting in Chief Lawrence intervening. After gathering the facts, the police chief permitted Lewis to leave with his son.

It's unclear how Lewis felt towards Charlie, but it's hard to imagine that Lewis liked the guy after he took his wife and child. What's perhaps odder is a quick newspaper mention that "before Albert's marriage to Emma, the sisters of Lewis Fowler's wife lived with Albert for several years."

While this perhaps implied a romantic relationship, according to the U..S Census, Lottie and Kittie Haight were born in 1868 and 1876, respectively, meaning that when Albert married Emma in 1879, the Haight sisters were only 11 and 3 years old. Albert's relationship with the Haight family remains unknown.

Assuming Emma Montfort wasn't a nudist, it's strange that none of her clothing was at the house where she lived with her husband and child. It is unclear who Mr. Lenihan, Emma Montfort's second husband, was and how their marriage happened, especially within a few months of Albert's passing.

Perhaps even more shocking is that according to New York City Marriage Records, on July 29, 1899, Emma remarried again! It's unclear what happened to Mr. Lenihan, but after a few short years of marriage, the former Emma Jean Reynolds-Montfort-Lenihan became Mrs. John Henry Hutt.

Despite Albert's neighbor Leonard Farrington admitting to ownership of the weapon used to commit the gruesome murder, his simple alibi that someone stole the ax from his woodpile that Sunday afternoon was enough to convince police he had nothing to do with the crime.

The man who found the bloody ax, Richard Robbins, used to live with Albert's first wife, Anne, when he was a teenager. It's unclear what their relationship was, but Anne tried to take ownership of his property after Albert's death. While that may all be a coincidence, there's something else.

In 1877, Leonard Farrington reported a strange occurrence. A stranger appeared at his house asking for a place to stay. Later in the night, an accomplice in a wagon mysteriously showed up. Sensing something wasn't right, Farrington chased the men away with a bayonet. Were they going to rob him? Murder him? The men escaped into the night, never identified.

Perhaps in an eerie coincidence, in December 1884, locals found the dead body of a man hanging to a tree near the site of the unsolved murder in Montfort's Woods. At first, investigators thought the victim, who was stripped completely nude, was a suicide. After further investigation, however, they ruled it was a case of robbery and murder. They determined the unidentified man was killed elsewhere and then taken to this spot in a wagon. Investigators found wagon wheel tracks leading out of Montfort's Woods, near the house where Albert once lived and was murdered.

13.) IN BETWEEN DAYS

A glimpse of Kensico life during the 1880s.

I

 In June 1883, a tramp that went by the name "McGowan" randomly attacked a dairy farmer named Jason Reynolds. During the ambush, Jason yelled to his wife for help. She appeared on the scene brandishing metal carriage spring. "McGowan" was later treated for severe head wounds.

II

 In June of 1884, a man named Silas Louden, a successful shoemaker became the talk of the town. He lived with his wife and children and regularly attended the Methodist Church, where Reverend Lane had become locally infamous for a kissing scandal. He met a young and pretty girl named Maggie Reynolds at the church.

 Several locals witnessed Silas and Maggie kissing. After some time, Maggie went to Silas' house and asked to stay. Silas provided her with a room on the upper floor of his house, and he also took a room on the same floor. However, Silas' wife becomes suspicious and orders the girl to leave. After Maggie left, Silas also left the house.

III

On a Monday afternoon that June, four intoxicated Kensico Dam workers went into the Joseph Reevs Hotel in town. The bartender, Samuel Robbins, kicked out the rowdy bunch. Instead of leaving, the drunken men attacked the bartender with chairs, clubs, and a knife. The assailants fled. Dr. Maxwell found Robbins' skull was fractured and that he had also received several wounds and contusions. The police arrested two of the assailants, who gave their names as "Collins" and "Monahan". The other two escaped on a train headed to New York City.

IV

That October, Thomas Hart's 5-year-old son Joseph went to bed on a typical Saturday night in Kensico. The following morning, he was found dead. Coroner Tice performed a post-mortem examination and determined the boy had consumed poisonous berries.

V

On Monday November 3, 1884, a 60-year-old Kensico farmer named John Donnelly walked to White Plains, had some drinks, and after becoming too intoxicated to walk home, slept in a barn.

The barn belonging to Ziba Carpenter facing Owaumpum Street in White Plains has a window even with the floor. Early the following morning, Donnelly fell out of the window. Unhurt, he picked himself up and began to walk home. Constable Bogart stopped him, examined him, and let him proceed without seeing any bruises or injuries.

He arrived in Kensico after dark that Tuesday night in a battered and dazed condition. There was a long, deep gash on the side of his head, his eyes were blackened, and there were several other bruises on his head and face. He told his wife and adult daughters, whom he lived with, a rambling story that inferred that despite having no money or valuables, he had been assaulted and beaten by robbers. The next morning, his family found him dead.

Coroner Tice performed an autopsy and determined he suffered a concussion of the brain. John Donnelly's murder remains unsolved.

VI

An eerie blurb appeared on the pages of the *Tri-States Union* newspaper in 1885:

"Kensico, Westchester County, has a haunted house. Moans, flashing lights, and terrible shrieks are the accompaniments."

Perhaps even more eerie is to remember that Trick-or-Treating didn't catch on in America until the 1930s, haunted attractions designed for fun scares didn't begin in the U.S. until the early 1900s, and the Port Jervis, NY- based newspaper printed this in the second week of December.

VII

One day in 1886, upon returning home after a long day at work, farmer Samuel Stevens discovered a peculiar note in Harrison, NY. His wife, Susan, wrote the message, "Dear Sam, I have gone, never to return." That same day, William Henry Garthwaite, a wealthy contractor from Kensico, disappeared.

 Samuel frantically searched for his wife and eventually discovered from witnesses that she had left with the couple's children in Mr. Garthwaite's buggy.

 Samuel knew W.H. and first met him four months earlier, shortly after the town of Harrison awarded W.H. a contract to construct a road from St. Mary's Lake (now Silver Lake) to Rye Lake. After receiving payment for the project, W.H. rented two rooms on the road between White Plains and Purchase, NY, close to the job site—one for his blacksmith Purdy Ackerly and his wife and the other for himself. In exchange for the room, the Acklery couple provided W.H. with nightly dinners. Both rooms were located in the house of Samuel Stevens.

 While staying at the house, the 50-year-old contractor, described as being about 5'8" and stout with a heavy mustache, became acquainted with Samuel's wife, Susan. Susan, a 21-year-old married mother of two, quickly decided to leave her husband and made plans with W.H. to elope.

VIII

In April 1886, W.H.'s blacksmith, Purdy Ackerly, had a run-in with two men at a bar. Purdy was a young married man in his mid-30s known for his hard work, musical talent as a violinist, and his son George. The two other men, Frederick Cunningham and Michael Burnett were known troublemakers in the area. They followed Purdy out of the bar, looking for a fight.

Ackerly slipped into an outhouse to avoid them, but they followed him and flipped the shed over, leaving Acklery with a broken back, an injury that killed him. The police eventually arrested and charged Cunningham and Burnett with murder.

IX

Kensico residents enjoyed George Mead's regionally famous fresh-baked bread, made daily at The Old Bakery on nearby Railroad Avenue in White Plains. George was well-known in town and was the man who discovered that Albert Montfort had been murdered.

One night in late January 1887, George and his wife socially visited with their neighbors. The Meads' sons, 14-year-old George Jr. and 23-year-old William, were left to operate the bakery while they were gone.

Around 9:15 pm, two hooligans ran into the store and ordered the 14-year-old to "stick 'em up!" George Jr. bravely ignored the robbers and screamed to alert his older brother, who was in an adjoining room. William burst into the store and tackled the large hoodlum. The scuffle spilled onto the street and caused a commotion and broken glass.

Witnesses on the road couldn't intervene before one of the hooligans displayed a revolver and shot William at close range. William, still clinging to his killer, yelled, "Murder!" before dropping dead.

The nearby witnesses chased the hooligans, who ran off towards Chatterton Hill. A posse of enraged locals and the police hunted the criminals to the shadows of some trees. Cornered near an arched bridge, the criminals drew their revolvers and fired at the police.

Despite the gunfire, the police continued their pursuit. Fearing arrest or lynching, the pair of desperados then pressed their guns to their own heads and shot. One died seconds later, while the other a few hours later in the County Jail hospital.

 The police discovered the hoodlums were carrying an additional Smith & Wesson, a .44 caliber, and an English Bulldog .32 caliber revolver, with innumerable ammunition. Each had a double-edged eight-inch dirk knife fasted to his suspended by a piece of a wire. A black silk mask and a total of 36 cents were found in their pockets.

 After reading about the tragic event in the newspaper, two young men from New York City dressed much like the pair that was lying dead in White Plains, showed up at the police station. They identified the deceased as their younger brothers, ages 17 and 19.

William's funeral was attended by the largest number of people ever within the walls of Memorial M.E. Church in White Plains. The Reverend concluded the services by saying, "But the suppression of crime will not be reached alone by carnal weapons or by the arm of the law. Unmoral and criminally sensational literature should also be suppressed. White Plains might well take the lead of rural towns."

X

In order to create space for Kensico's new lake, some localities had to be destroyed. The Public Works department paid large sums of money to residents, such as Joseph Tompkins for dismantling his sawmill, Oliver Matthews for two pieces of land on Big Rye Pond, and Frank Tilford for damage to his stock and dairy farm on Big Rye Pond. Public Works granted an additional $9,592 to the Westchester Ice Company.

When workers completed the original Kensico Dam around 1886, the villagers took advantage of becoming a lakeside town. The Raven family reopened their hotel at its new location. Now known as The Lake View Hotel, the Orchard Street venue grew popular with workers from the dam who enjoyed drinking in the hotel saloon. Despite many of the strict Methodists in town disliking the establishment because they served beer, wine, and hard liquor, the lakeside hotel attracted people who enjoyed fishing, boating, and ice skating on the lake.

Caroline Raven would find employees for the family's establishment by going to Ellis Island. The Ravens usually hired people from their native Germany because they could easily communicate. Other Kensico farmers also hired laborers at New York City's Battery Park.

Being a fresh lakeside town took some adjusting. Later, in 1886, a 22-year-old truck driver dove off the road into Kensico Lake with about $10,000 worth of print goods. A derrick retrieved the truck and cargo several hours after the thrilling plunge.

The town's central meeting place became Pfister's store. The former Odell Store, taken over by Mr. Bang and now owned by Jacob Pfister, offered almost everything the valley's farm families needed, including flour, sugar, nails, and kerosene for lamps in the non-electrified village. Mr. Pfister also served as postmaster for the town's 200 - 250 residents. A horse-drawn stagecoach stopped at his store twice a day in each direction. He would hand the stage driver a bag of outgoing letters each day, each carrying his stamp "Kensico, N.Y."

Farmer Clark Ryder opened a store on the other side of the crossroads. He spent most of his time working on his farm and was alerted of customers by a woman upstairs hollering out the window. Then, Mr. Ryder would stroll through the back door, his boots likely decorated with manure. Ryder took pride in being a Democrat in a small Republican community.

Willis Husted was the local horse specialist and owner of the first steam press cider mill near Bill Miller's grist mill and the Reynolds family's dairy farm. Numerous new hotels sprung up in town, including Koch's Crystal Spring Hotel on King Street and Myrtle's Summer Hotel, operated by the Greenops brothers. Many establishments served liquor, including the popular Lane's Saloon.

A reporter visiting Kensico in 1887 wrote:

"There are more gin mills in Kensico than any place of its size in Westchester County. Four are kept open on Sundays, regardless of the law. They sell their liquors and beer and then have a free fight. Sometimes, these brawlers are arrested, and then the complaint is

thrown out of court, and their Justices of the Peace and other men of good church-standing shield them from the law. This place has been the scene of two murders, store-keeper Albert Montfort and Purdy Ackerly, which occurred last summer. This was a drunken carousal on Sunday. A great many families have moved away to civilization. We would say in closing that we hope at the next Spring election, they will vote no-license and that these taverns will be abolished and peace and quietness reign supreme."

Kensico men voted for local elections on the second floor of Joe Carpenter's blacksmith shop near Ryder's store and next to a schoolhouse. Dolly Merritt taught at the school and enjoyed teaching children about the Revolutionary War and its local events. Little did they know, some of their most significant local events were still yet to come.

XI

In May 1889, a 53-year-old veteran of the New York Volunteers, Charles Wintston, was killed after a load of whitewood logs crushed him. He was drawing the wood for a White Plains lumberyard. The accident occurred in Montfort's Woods, just below Archer's Hill, which locals say is the resting place of sachems Pathungo and Cokenencko.

XII

In January 1891, farmer Hiram Gale's sons were considered three of the brightest boys in town. 20-year-old Harry, 13-year-old Eugene, and 10-year-old Frank enjoyed ice skating on the frozen lake.

One night, the two eldest Gale brothers skated towards the lake's center while Frank hung out with friends near the shoreline. The ice cracked. As they shouted for help, numerous others rushed toward the center of the lake, but as they got close, the ice began to break, and they couldn't reach the boys, who drowned in the frozen waters.

14.) THE FARMER & THE OUTLAW

Henry Woodman operated a large farm on the outskirts of town on the old Route 22 near Archer's Hill. Known for having the nicest farmhouse and best cattle in the area, the well-to-do bachelor in his 50s lived with his two unmarried sisters. The Woodman women say that on Saturday morning, April 11, 1891, their brother mysteriously vanished..

The ladies say their brother left the house that morning with a lot of money in his pockets and was last seen by Squire Archer around 6 pm, exiting his place and taking the road toward the lakes. Wagon wheel marks were traced to the edge of Little Rye Lake, where the trail ends.

Squire Archer's boat, which he left docked near the bank of the lake, was found in the water, about 50 feet out. Some believe Henry tried crossing the lake in the boat and accidentally drowned, but other townspeople think someone murdered Henry Woodman. After the recent unsolved deaths of Albert Montfort, farmer John Donnelly, and the unidentified man found hanging to a tree in Montfort's Woods, folks in Kensico became fearful of a killer on the loose.

A week after Henry's disappearance, local men dragged the lake for his body. They didn't find anything. The men tried again a few days later and were also unsuccessful.

On May 9, nearly one month after Henry's disappearance, two Kensico Reservoir employees spotted something floating in Little Rye Lake. William Glenning and Effingham Ferris pulled Henry's corpse from the water.

The coroner determined there were no marks of violence on the body and concluded Henry Woodman's death to be an accident, though villagers kept their suspicions otherwise.

The water where the men discovered Henry Woodman's body is behind modern-day Park Lane, the road that on one end connects to Old Orchard Street and on the other runs towards New York's most haunted street, Buckout Road. The outlet of water was later renamed Woodman's Cove.

A few weeks later, one of the dam workers who pulled Henry Woodman's body from the lake, William Glenning, went on a violent rampage. Armed with a revolver and a shotgun, Glenning went into town looking for a fight. Luckily, nobody in town got hurt, but then Glenning stormed into the gatehouse at the south end of Kensico Reservoir.

William Glenning pointed his revolver at employees Samuel Lawrence and John Daly. "Throw up your hands!" he shouted. He then demanded they leave their station and permit him to have control. He said the city needed more water; therefore, he would control the reservoir gates.

The employees tried to ration with him, but he wouldn't back down. A third employee entered the station, causing Glenning to take his aim off, Daly and Lawrence. With Glenning locked in on a new target, Lawrence seized the opportunity and bravely smacked the gunman's revolver out of his hand and across the floor. They secured the disarmed trespasser and let him back loose outside the Kensico streets.

A little while later, Mr. Glenning reappeared, demanding the return of his pistol. Mr. Daly and Mr. Lawrence ignored the maniac. Glenning responded angrily by making violent death threats and displaying a shotgun. Daly and Lawrence then assured him that his revolver was being returned to his local residence, and after seeing an opportunity to escape, the two spooked employees bolted.

Running for their lives, the frightened workers found safety with Constable Bogart. That evening, Bogart, police officer Davidson, and a few amateur self-proclaimed bounty hunters gathered in Kensico to apprehend Mr. Glenning.

The posse successfully arrested Glenning, who felt he did nothing wrong. The police were familiar with him as he had previously gotten into similar trouble. They say he suffers from a condition where he believes that he is famous western gunslinger Buffalo Bill. Mr. Glenning thinks that in holding up men and terrorizing a whole village, he is only doing what the famous western cowboy does every day as a pastime.

As this battle ended, another was about to start. Commissioner Daly, the new man in charge of the Department of Public Works, was about to launch a war on microbes.

15.) THE NEW POLLUTION

Commissioner Daly's quest was inspired by the discoveries made by European doctors about germs in drinking water. In 1854, a London doctor named John Snow proved that cholera spread through contaminated drinking water and discovered that after human sewage had contaminated a water well, it caused the spread of cholera, resulting in 616 deaths. Around the same time, scientists such as Louis Pasteur from France and Robert Koch from Germany proposed the idea that germs cause diseases and can spread through untreated water.

Governments responded by taking action to ensure their drinking water supplies were safe. At first, efforts focused on removing microbiological contaminants such as protozoan, bacteriological, or viral contaminants. They tried to prevent raw sewage from entering bodies of water used as sources of drinking water and treated water taken from lakes, rivers, and reservoirs.

New York opened the world's first municipal laboratory, the Bacteriological Laboratory, in 1892, routinely identifying diseases. A year later, in New York City, The Department of Public Works determined that numerous pollutants were entering Kensico's reservoir, causing contamination of New York City's drinking water. To battle this problem, Commissioner Daly launched what he called "The War on Microbes."

Armed with the authority to evict residents and destroy property when necessary, in 1893, Commissioner Daly and his comrades began inspecting areas of the village that were creating the problem. Despite violators receiving some compensation for any destruction, the crusading party attracted considerable negative attention when they arrived in town. Villagers angrily watched as Daly and his men made their rounds, inspecting numerous properties within 250 feet of the water's edge.

Jennie Gardner, a widow, was found to have violated several rules. She had a pig pen, a hen coop, and an outhouse on the unwalled edge of the reservoir. When Commissioner Daly inspected her property, he informed her that the little house she lived in would have to be relocated. Jennie expressed not having the funds to relocate. Commissioner Daly granted her three months to find a new home.

When Daly visited the estate of Evander Odell, he shockingly observed a large barn stuffed with filth and manure near the reservoir's edge. Daly ordered the immediate removal of the poop and the destruction of the building within three days.

Next door to Mr. Odell's poop heap and also on the reservoir's unwalled edge were neighbor Uriah Robinson's outhouses, pigpens, and chicken coops. Next to him was the pigpen, manure pile, and outhouse of H.P. Fisher, which were so close to the neighboring schoolhouse that its pupils could also enjoy its aroma.

The school had several flooded outbuildings within 150 feet of the water and close to the foul manure heap of Charles Wykoff, whose store, with its yard trimmed with refuse, adjoined the Methodist

Church. Daly ordered removing all of the outhouses.

Daly discovered that the liquor shop belonging to John Wykoff was operating out of another man's filthy horse stable. It was right on the edge of Rye Creek next to a small building he owned, with a cellar half filled with water, that he used as a closet. Daly ordered it all destroyed.

Despite immediately finding several violations, Daly told residents, "It is not true that I intend to wipe out Kensico. It is nonsense to say that this removal will wipe out the town."

Wesley Robbins and his family lived in a building that Daly considered old and unstable and ordered its destruction. Additionally, Daniel Brundage's house was also condemned and destroyed. Brundage commented, "I thought this house might be carried away someday by a flood."

A wealthy farmer named Daniel Tucker lived nearby and expressed frustration to a *New York Times* reporter, saying, "I've lived here for thirty years, long before New York was anything. Why did they suddenly come down on us and tell us these houses must be demolished?"

The reporter, noticing Tucker's property, asked, "How long have those houses on the stream's bank been occupied?"

The farmer replied, "About seven years."

"And for seven years," the reporter pointed out, "these nuisances have existed!"

Moments later, Commissioner Daly told the angry farmer that his stable, situated on the water's edge and had accumulated a significant amount of filth, must be cleaned out immediately.

"All right," the farmer said.

Stephen Gale's barn hangs over the edge of Bear Gutter Creek, and the accompanying manure heap that he had been piling up since the winter was near spilling into the water. Even worse was what Daly found at A.C. Acklery's Brookside Hotel.

What he described as a "little fourth-rate hostelry" is on the other side of the road but is so close to the brook that the foundations are washed by the water when the stream is full. The hotel's refuse spills into the streams, as does the adjoining outhouse. Daly's men proposed to burn the place immediately because it was so foul, but Commissioner Daly granted Ackerly two days to vacate.

The last stop of the day was the home of Jonathan Tompkins. Worth an estimated $100,000 (worth about $3.5 Million today), the descendent of former New York Governor Warren Tompkins lived in a house near the Kensico Hotel.

Mr. Tompkins was unfazed by the negative comments thrown his way by his neighbors, who were following Commissioner Daly and the inspectors. One neighbor claimed that Mr. Tompkins had something putrid in his barn. When one of Daly's workers kicked open the barn door, they found a dead horse on a pile of straw. The floorboards were rotten and covered in slime. The smell of the decomposing horse filled the air as the workers removed it by wagon. Daly noticed the barn was on the brook's edge and ordered demolition.

While Daly's crew went at it with crowbars and axes, a neighbor told Daly that the old house next to it was even worse. Tompkins declared the place deserted, but Daly quickly discovered it was actually the house the old miser resided in.

An investigation proved this place to be the most vile dwelling inspected. From the cellar to the attic, Mr. Tompkins filled the house with ashes, tomato cans, scraps of iron, old rags, decaying vegetables, and other ill-smelling items.

Inspectors could hardly enter the second level due to the vast rubbish and garbage occupying its two rooms. A filthy feather mattress adorned the floor of one room. The bedding and pillow were so dirty that they were black. In the other room were several hundred old tin cans, a stove, and filth of every description. On one side of the room was a bureau with an old clock.

As villagers told reporters that Mr. Tompkins was the meanest man in Kensico and lived on a mere $7 a month, he watched on. Dressed in dirty clothes and a shaggy old fur cap layered with dust, he politely answered questions in a well-spoken manner. After Commissioner Daly discovered numerous pails containing water and soaking bones, Mr. Tompkins explained that he enjoyed a good soup.

Mr. Daly told Mr. Tompkins he could take anything from the house other than the old rags, bedding, or bones, as he did not want any disease spreading throughout the village. He said he wanted the old clock. Villagers theorized that's where he hid his money.

After grabbing his clock, Mr. Daly ordered the property set on fire. Bundles of hay were piled against the house, then set ablaze with a match. As the villagers watched the house go up in flames, Mr. Tompkins tried to re-enter the burning building, claiming he had forgotten to take something out of a drawer in the bureau.

Deputy Sheriff Stanfield, perhaps feeling empathy, climbed into the second-story window, retrieved the drawer, and jumped to the ground. As the house burned to the ground, the village elder who once gave the town its name walked away into the night, carrying his old clock.

16.) THE OLD MAIN DRAG

Daily life in Kensico during 1893 was far from dull. Normalcy resumed after Commissioner Daly left town, but in typical Kensico fashion, it didn't take long for things to be disrupted by fresh ideas, mystery, and tragedies.

A few days after Commissioner Daly ordered the removal of outhouse waste and manure piles from the reservoir's edge, *The Dobbs Ferry Register* reported a story about a local Kensico farmer's new business venture.

"A syndicate has been organized to operate the large mineral springs at Kensico. The farm on which the springs were found was bought for a huge price. The company hopes to procure one thousand barrels daily, and they talk of naming it Kensico Water."

It's unclear whether or not this early idea for mineral water came to fruition.

In the fall, a Connecticut man named Mr. Pickhard came to Kensico to hang posters at the local post office bearing a sketch of his missing daughter. 15-year-old Clara had mysteriously vanished. The frantic father and local police had been unable to find her. He feared there may have been foul play involved or that she committed suicide. Luckily, postmaster Pfister had a lead.

Mr. Pfister sent the frightened father to talk with a man in town named

Fred Powers. Mr. Powers said a girl answering Clara's description called his house at midnight Tuesday and inquired how far it was to the Kensico station on Harlem Road. She was well-dressed and refused to come in. The following day, she returned and purchased a ticket to New York.

The same morning, a young man called for a drink at the Kensico Hotel bar, saying he had been out all night. When Clara's dad heard a description of the man, he thought it might be someone Clara had known who had just recently returned to town from Chicago, leading him to believe they had eloped. It's unclear what happened to Clara, though some witnesses think they spotted her working in New York City and said she ran away because her father was too strict.

A few weeks later, the Harlem Milk Train fatally struck 21-year-old Patrick Carr. The accident happened near Kensico Station. Locals said the victim was intoxicated.

Sadly, just weeks after the accident, the train fatally struck another local man. Returning home from Grand Central Station, Frank Anderson, who was in his 40s, was found killed after being struck by a northbound train in Bronxville. The victim had a train ticket, a gold watch, and bills for hardware and nails that he had purchased.

In December 1893, the final water tunnel to Kensico broke ground. Tammany Hall politician John McQuade was the contractor, and over 200 men worked on the project. The tunnel aims to divert the Byram River into the Kensico Reservoir. Unfortunately, that December, there was a terrible accident.

On December 9, a dynamite explosion in the tunnel blew two man into fragments. At least five workers received severe injuries, some life-threatening. The explosion occurred soon after 5 pm, just after the men on the night shift had begun work. The men had no warning of what was to happen.

The explosion blew up the dynamite house, causing debris and stones to fall and fill the mouth of the tunnel. The unsuspecting workers heard an unknown rumbling noise followed by a loud explosion boom, which residents heard for miles.

Immediately after the shock, the miners came rushing out of the tunnel. Most of the men working on the job site are Italian and are only known by numbers. The people in charge couldn't confirm whether all the workers had been accounted for. When seen at his home on Lexington Ave later that night, Contractor McQuade had no knowledge that the explosion happened.

About two years later, the Italian workers spoke out in large numbers. The men who worked on the tunnel connecting the Byram River to Bear Gutter Creek formed a mob to protest due to issues with their wages. Contractor McQuade eventually resolved the situation after a considerable amount of rioting.

17.) NEW DIRECTION

After the village of Kensico was used to address New York City's drinking water problem, the small farming village soon tried to remedy another of the city's issues. The Children's Aid Society of New York had been troubled with what's best to do with troublesome teenage boys, and a wealthy New Yorker named Mrs. White had a solution.

Mrs. Joseph White bought a 125-acre farm on the outskirts of Kensico. She donated the property and $10,000 to the Children's Aid Society. The group plans to have troubled New York City teens shipped up the railroad to board at the facility for several months at a clip. While there, principal farmers will be on hand to direct the boys' efforts, teaching them farming techniques. The farmers will sell the produce raised at the school, which will help fund the school. Billed as "a place where boys can learn how to become men," the Brace Memorial Farm School at Kensico proudly opened in 1894.

Builders made the three-storied school modeled after the old Colonial-style farmhouses, with broad porches supported by old-fashioned white columns. The large and spacious school accommodates about 100 boys. A dorm for the students is on the top floor, and additional rooms for staff are on the second floor. The first floor has a school room, offices, a dining room, kitchen, laundry, and bathrooms. The interior is finished in pine wood and has exceptional lighting. The site also has a barn.

The school's first incoming students were twenty teens from a New York City homeless shelter. They welcomed the idea of sleeping on a real bed and having the opportunity to learn new skills. Upon arrival, the boys are issued uniforms: overalls with matching jumpers and heavy shoes. Within a few months, the school's student population doubled, and continued to grow.

Despite being presented as a school that would host children voluntarily, the facility became known locally as "The Orphan Asylum." On numerous occasions, "inmates" tried to escape, often by descending a second-story window and climbing down intertwined bed sheets. The police and school authorities would work together to bring the children back.

In a particular case, two 14-year-olds named John Riley and John White decided to leave their farming occupation. They didn't have any intention to cause trouble, but they were apprehended by the police. Upon questioning, they explained to the arresting officers that they were required to wake up at 4 am and work until 8 pm, and they simply did not enjoy farming.

After a few years, the school added barbed wire fences around its perimeter. The prison-like installments didn't stop five eager students, Ferdinand Steen, James Riggon, Benjamin Kelly, Joseph Pompadour, and Eugene Krauser, from busting out.

The group of teens, aged 14-19, made it to New York City, where the police stopped them. While at police headquarters, they told the officers they had no interest in learning to be farmers, and since they were there voluntarily, they should be permitted to leave on their own accord; one student commented, "The school wasn't what it was cracked up to be."

Eventually, the routine of students escaping, being arrested, and returning to school ceased. The police did, however, make one more arrest at the Brace Farming School, and it was shocking: the school's superintendent.

A student named Thomas Barnshaw accused the school's superintendent, Charles Fisher, of assault. The boy said that Mr. Fisher hit him and kept him penned up all day in the guardhouse. The school's equivalent to a prison's solitary confinement cell, the Brace students referred to it as "The Coffin Stretcher."

The entire student population attended Mr. Fisher's trial. Dressed in their school uniforms, the boys eagerly listened as a staff member testified against Mr. Fisher, stating he witnessed assaults, including Fisher handcuffing a boy. He also testified that the "food is uniformly and dangerously bad" and said that in one night, 29 boys had gotten food poisoning.

The proceedings also revealed that the school's farmers had not examined its cows for tuberculosis, resulting in the students drinking contaminated milk.

After several days of testimony, the jury failed to reach a unanimous verdict. Mr. Fisher was released, though the judge ordered the destruction of "The Coffin Stretcher."

18.) TRAIN IN VAIN

The train line had a positive impact on the prosperity of the farming village, but it also posed a significant danger as there were frequent fatalities. In 1897, W.G. Harper, a florist from Kensico, and one of his employees named Samuel Smith lost their lives immediately after being hit by the Pittsfield Express while crossing the tracks. Unfortunately, a catastrophic disaster was looming on the horizon.

In front of Kensico Station around 8:40 pm on August 21, 1900 there was a terrible collision. The southbound freight train pulled into the station around 8 pm. While sitting idle on the rails, a second train, loaded with ice, smashed into it.

The debris buried the 40-year-old engineer, William Lauterbach, and 35-year-old fireman, Henry Cassidy, of the ice train, crushing them to death. The collision also claimed the lives of 30-year-old brakeman William Abel and another unidentified man. Removing wreckage became challenging because tons of ice piled all over the smashed train cars.

Kensico resident Robert Ross saw the incoming train and the inevitable disaster. He immediately ran to help flag down an incoming train to help the injured.

Six train cars had to be burned to clear the tracks, and over 150 tons of ice and 2,000 bushels remained strewn about the tracks for several days. An undertaker in White Plains handled arrangements for the deceased. Searches were unable to recover the brakeman's decapitated head.

In March 1901, the Harlem Railroad contracted a couple of hundred workers to build a double-track extension between White Plains and Mt. Kisco on the railroad tracks. Most of these workers were Italian and moved into a row of shanty houses in Kensico.

The contractors who owned the houses established that all the laborers must be in their huts by 10 pm. They hired night watchmen, including a guard named Pietro Notali, to enforce this rule.

One Monday evening in mid-March, a situation arose between Notali and the workers' foreman, Dom Sambastino. There are different versions of how the quarrel began; one starts with the men drinking beer together in a hut and arguing over who should pay for more beer, while another leans more towards Mr. Notali, preventing Mr. Sambastino from entering his sleeping quarters.

Regardless of how the situation began, it ended with Mr. Notali shooting Mr. Sambastino at close range with a shotgun. The charge struck the victim's mouth, causing instant death. Mr. Notali fled into the woods.

The next day, around 300 Italian workers went on strike to protest the unnecessary murder of their boss. Many of the workers were frustrated that they had to pay $7 a month for boarding, regardless of whether they used the bungalows or not. Some had homes and either paid the fee without staying in the huts or downgraded their living conditions to stay in the shanties.

The strikers threatened to burn the huts to the ground. A contingent of the group procured a rope and threatened to lynch the murderer. The large group hunted for Mr. Notali throughout the woods of Kensico, Stony Hill, and Cranberry Lake. The mob next patrolled the railroad tracks and threatened to kill any laborer who raised a pick or shovel. A group of women followed the rioters, cursing the killer.

When the deputies arrived to calm the situation, many of the rioters were brandishing knives and revolvers. They complained that they had only received sums of about sixty cents for the whole month's work and would choose to sleep in the woods instead of in the huts. Despite police calming the situation, they kept deputies on guard for several nights as the mob continued searching for the murderer.

It's unclear what became of Mr. Notali. That May, the Harlem Railroad fatally struck an unnamed Italian man on the tracks at Kensico. Reports say he was engaged with some Italian laborers on the railway.

19.)I AM THE RESURRECTION

In August 1901, a freak accident killed a local farmer named Oscar Purdy. While on his way back to his Kensico home, his horses got frightened, resulting in Mr. Purdy being thrown from his carriage, breaking his neck and fracturing his skull.

The married father was a victim of a robbery several years prior. A young man stole several chickens from Mr. Purdy's property. Mr. Purdy responded by apprehending the thief with a shotgun. He chose not to press charges, thinking the thief learned his lesson.

While Mr. Purdy was a well-respected and hardworking community member, his neighbor, J. Luther Pierson, was among the village's most controversial.

In 1901, two of Mr. Pierson's young children died in succession from pneumonia. After his two-month-old son, Earl, died at the Pierson's home in Kensico, the police got involved. They arrested Mr. Pierson because he neglected to provide either child with medicine. Mr. Pierson's defense, however, is that he is a "Faith Curist."
Instead of permitting their children to attend public school, the Piersons hired a private instructor. Mr. Pierson strictly rejected the idea of using traditional medicine of any kind. After Earl's death, the police fined him $530. Instead of paying the fine, Mr. Pierson went to jail.

While locked up in White Plains, the warden, Joe Pye, said Pierson tried to convert the prisoners to his beliefs. The police released him after Pierson posted bail—$ 500. Mr. Pye said "If he had not been released, half the prisoners would have become his followers, as he seemed to hypnotize them with his talks on how to cure and heal by prayer."

When Mr. Pierson returned home to Kensico, his followers met him at his family's residence, locally known as The Overlook. While Catholic mass was in session at the nearby church, Mr. Pierson conducted a private service for his faith curist congregation members.

Pierson spoke about his future plans:

"I expect to go back to my desk in the accounting department of the New York Central Railroad company on Monday. The company has employed me for ten years and expects to hold my position just the same as I have received no word to the contrary. A man has a right to his religious beliefs, and they should not interfere with his business. I shall not run away; that is a certainty."

Living at the house with the Pierson family was a 68-year-old woman, Mrs. Ford, known to fellow Faith Curists as Sister Ford. Mrs. Ford died in the Pierson home after not being treated for a prolonged illness, later revealed as cystitis.

Later that day, Pierson posted a sign to the front door of The Overlook: "This house for sale. Furniture for sale, cheap." In October 1903, Pierson avoided trial by fully paying his fine—$ 530.
A year later, Christina LaQuint's dog ran onto the railroad tracks as the young local girl waited for the train at Kensico Station. The girl had

driven her dog off the southbound track just as a local train shot by and was crossing the northbound path when the express engine was speeding towards her. When she reached the center of the tracks, she stood frozen.

The train tossed her thirty feet, and she landed in a ditch in a mangled form. Horrified witnesses recalled that "only a short time ago, her brother was scalded to death at Kensico."

In the spring of 1904, Nelson Brown took the train from his hometown, Kensico, to White Plains to look for work. He brought with him his resume, addressed to the Superintendent of the Prudential Life Insurance Company.

After his interview, he realized he didn't have enough money to take the train home to Kensico. He started walking up the track in the blinding rain. A speeding train fatally struck him. Investigators found his body. The contents in his pockets included part of a letter addressed to F.F. Ford, the Prudential Life Insurance Company superintendent.

A speeding train also struck 55-year-old farmer Walter Klingham as he walked along the tracks at Kensico. He was placed on the next southbound train and taken to the White Plains. Perhaps even more surprising than his miraculous recovery was when he mentioned to the doctor that this wasn't the first time he had been hit by a train.

20.)   LEAVE HOME

The early 1900s were an exciting time for people in Kensico. Much like their Revolutionary War ancestors, they had grown up without electricity, telephones, airplanes, or automobiles.

In 1902, developers built the area's first stone road. It ran from the Oak Tree Inn in North White Plains (Save Way Cleaners location in modern times) to Cooney Road in Kensico. Before this, Kensico only had dirt roads and narrow wagon trails. The townsfolk sensed significant changes on the horizon but were shocked by the news they received in 1905.

Increasingly fearful of drought and disease, New York City required even more water than the original Kensico Reservoir could provide. The city needed a larger water supply and quickly won approval from the state legislature to take the land required for the project from the village of Kensico.

The horrifying news quickly spread around the village. The new Kensico Dam would dwarf the present one that was built less than twenty years prior. Two thousand two hundred acres of Kensico would be flooded and covered by 30 billion gallons of water.

Initially, the plan was to construct the new dam in front of the old one. However, this plan had to be scrapped as insufficient solid rock was underneath to support the foundation. As a result, the developers pivoted and decided to build the new dam behind the old one, meaning they'd first have to drain the lake.

 The people were shocked when they saw the maps outlining a reservoir ten times larger than the small lake they knew. The dam, which was 1,800 feet long and 160 feet high, would raise the water level by an incredible 100 feet up the slopes of Reynolds Hill, Cooney Hill, and Ackerley's Hill. Archer's Hill, where the Archer family had farmed for generations, would be turned into an island.

 The new dam would flood the Rye Ponds completely and cover almost all the hillside farms. Churches, schools, stores, and homes would be destroyed. The crossroads where George Washington's officers met, the barn where The Continental Army detained Charles Lee and Major Andre, and the house George Washington used as a Revolutionary War headquarters would be underwater.

 After the first Kensico Dam was built in the 1880s, followed by Commissioner Daly's "War on Microbes" in the 1890s, the village didn't try to stop these new plans. They knew they couldn't do anything to stop it, despite life as they knew it literally being destroyed.

 In 1906, the state of New York approved the final plans for the massive project. Workers built a seventeen-mile railroad and a small network of roads to carry building materials from the Collins Quarry near Cranberry Lake to the dam construction site.

 In preparation for the construction of the new Kensico Dam, Kensico Lake had to be drained along with a swamp that covered the area that is modern-day Kensico Dam Plaza. All property belonging to the people in the vicinity was condemned and then appraised. The city paid the owners what they deemed a fair value for the land.

The Raven family was the first to sell their land, but they did not sell their property to the city. Instead, they sold the Lake View Hotel to the Jennie Clarkson Home for Children. The city's new reservoir plans did not affect it since they had previously relocated the hotel to the highland on Old Orchard Street.

Mr. Raven stated, "I have raised all my children here. If the Jennie Clarkson people think it can help their children, they should have it." The hotel was utilized as a temporary children's home before a movie director destroyed it as a fiery prop for an early motion picture.

Despite being unable to change the inevitable evacuation of Kensico, day-to-day life marched forward, though perhaps slower than before. Of course, in Kensico, there were always a few eyebrow-raising events around the small town.

In 1906, the Town Supervisor, Joseph See, sold a collection of items accumulated in his office for over 20 years. These items included rings, pins, bags, revolvers, and clothing, which had been found on the bodies of deceased individuals during the coroner's inquests. None of the deceased's relatives had ever claimed these items.

A local man bought a gold band wedding ring marked "Lena Lehann". The buyer remembered finding that same ring 20 years prior when he was the coroner.

The ring was worn on the body of a man who had drowned in a pond near Kensico Station. Mr. Hopkins had turned over the ring with other personal effects to a relative of the drowning victim. Afterward, that relative was killed, and nobody claimed the items. Mr. Hopkins said he bought the ring as a souvenir.

That June, a group of young boys from the village went fishing at Kensico Lake. During the morning, all of the boys left the lake to get more bait, except for six-year-old William Ackerman who remained behind to fish from a rock on the edge of the lake. When his older brother and the other boys returned, they noticed Willie was missing, assuming he had gone home for dinner. However, when they arrived home without him, Mr. Ackerman immediately began a search for his son.

Searchers found Willie's fishing pole on the rock where he had been sitting. After grappling in the deep waters for over an hour, the child's body was recovered, within a few feet of where he fell in.

When John Wykoff moved to Connecticut in 1906, taking his family's name out of the village for the first time in a century, the church had to search for a new treasurer. Blacksmith Joe Carpenter's sister Belle headed the Ladies Aid Society. She recruited dairy herd farmer Frank Reynolds to fill the position. The two worked together and devised a plan that surprised the neighborhood: upgrading the Methodist Church.

Using church funds to repair a structure the city would destroy soon seemed silly to almost everyone in town. The fellas that hung out at

Pfister's store poked fun at Mr. Reynolds with sarcastic lines like "Here comes the Ladies Aid man!" and "He even believes in women's suffrage, and he spends money on a building that's going to be torn down."

Reynolds paid no attention to the trivial smack talk. Instead, with the Ladies Aid Society, they spent around $2,500 of the church's money to renovate the church's interior. They varnished the pews, purchased a new red carpet, installed a hot-air furnace, and replaced the old roof with a new one.

The local store jokers were stunned when the city commissioners agreed to pay $21,000 for the newly improved church property, a whopping 50 percent more than the original estimate.

New York City continued to pay landowners fair value for their Kensico property. In 1907, they even had to compensate a farmer whose cows had mistakenly eaten some of their workers' sticks of dynamite. After selling their homes, many of Kensico's residents relocated to neighboring towns, like the Ravens, who moved to Armonk.

Many of the buildings in Kensico were destroyed and burnt to the ground. However, some structures were carefully dismantled to preserve the wood and stone, which builders later used to construct new houses in Valhalla.

Many of the village's buildings were destroyed and burnt, but some structures were carefully dismantled so their wood and stone could be repurposed for new houses in neighboring Valhalla. After the final Sunday service at Kensico's Methodist Church, the bell and furnace were removed and relocated to the Valhalla Methodist Church. Its furniture was sent to Castle Heights Methodist Church in North White Plains.

By the end of 1909, Kensico's population had dwindled, and only a few farmers remained in the town. Before year's end, Jacob Pfister permanently closed the Kensico post office and moved his store to Valhalla.

The Kensico Dam project required building lots of tiny temporary homes, called camps, near the work site to accommodate nearly 2,000 workers and their families. Many of these camps sprung up nearby on North Broadway and Cloverdale Avenue in White Plains. On the west side of the lake, an additional site, Camp Columbus, had 43 more buildings to support 500 workers.

The New York Board of Water Supply purchased a home on nearby Nethermont Ave. They converted the house on the steep hill overlooking Old Orchard Street into a school for the children of the Kensico Dam workers. The school also held night classes for the workers, many of whom were Italian immigrants who didn't know how to read or write in English.

By the end of 1910, New York City had acquired all of the land that would become the Kensico Reservoir. One of the first projects for the workers was to drain and fill a large swamp to form the present Kensico Dam Plaza.

In the winter of 1910, just before Christmas, Kensico was hit by a snowstorm that left a layer of four-inch-thick ice on the lake, which still needed to be drained. The frozen lake caught students' attention from the recently renovated Jennie Clarkson Home on Old Orchard Street. Otto Hubenthal, the school's best ice skater, was especially eager to seize the opportunity to skate across the frozen lake.

The 15-year-old loved ice skating. "Aw, come on, let's try it. I bet I can make it back in ten minutes. No one game? Then, here goes alone. So long!" he shouted to his pals, who described him as the fastest skater in school.

Fifty of his classmates and nearly two thousand workers watched him dart across the ice at high speed. Otto spun over the ice, reached the center, and then his body shot down into a hole, never seen again. Workers and classmates watched in horror but could not rescue the boy due to the ice being so thin.

Rescue parties couldn't retrieve the teenager's body from the frozen reservoir. The cold weather prevented them from draining the lake, and they didn't use grappling hooks because the current may have already carried the body to another part of the water.

It's unclear whether or not rescuers ever recovered the body of the young boy, whom classmates described as well-liked in the village. There was no sign of Otto's body a year later when about a hundred fishermen and local boys gathered to help capture and relocate the lake's population of fish.

In November 1912, quarry workers set off fifteen tons of dynamite in one massive blast at the stone quarry on Old Orchard Street. They blew up the quarry to provide stone for the dam construction. The quarry covers several acres, and for more than a month, drillers have been boring 4-inch holes from 15 to 20 feet into the rock to contain the dynamite charges, 1,235 sticks in all. The explosion made a big noise and a big hole.

In addition to excavating the site for the new dam, workers built an entire infrastructure of roads and railroad tracks in the area. Horses, mules, steam shovels, and steam engines were the tools for the job. The small gauge railroad ran from Rye Lake to the quarry near Cranberry Lake, which workers used to transport sand, gravel, and granite to build the dam.

They developed a new road, called The New Route 22, from the job site to Armonk. They also constructed a small hospital at the northeast intersection of North Broadway and Hillandale Avenue in North White Plains. Town Supervisor Joseph See's home, on a knoll in Kensico, was taken for watershed purposes and repurposed as a community recreation center.

On a tragic day in April 1915, a premature dynamite explosion in a trench at the Kensico Dam site killed eight Italian workers and injured nearly a dozen more.

The loud roar from a dozen sticks of dynamite sent a 40-ton shower of rocks raining down on the men working 90 feet underground. Before they could reach a point of safety, the explosion blew them down to the bottom of the excavation, entirely covered with rock and fallen debris.

Foreman Juliano signaled a rescue crew to scramble and lower an emergency basket. One by one, they hoisted several of the injured men, five of whom were unconscious, to safety and rushed to the camp hospital in North White Plains.

Mounted police tried to keep order as word about the tragedy quickly spread. Concerned family members flocked to the scene, eager to see if they recognized the victims. By the use of derricks, Foreman Juliano's crew was able to retrieve the mangled bodies of the workers who didn't make it out alive.

While the reservoir filled, the architects continued their work on the detailed designs for the stone and brickwork on the upper and lower pavilions and fountains. A year later, on May 23, 1916, the new Kensico Reservoir reached its maximum capacity of 40 billion gallons.

Workers completed the Kensico Dam in 1917 for an estimated total cost of $15 million (approximately $319M in 2024). The dam is 1,825 feet long, stands 307 feet above its foundation, and contains 1,00,000 feet of masonry. It is capable of holding back about 30 billion gallons of water. Its size is comparable to the amount of masonry used in building some Egyptian pyramids.

The northern half of Kensico Reservoir is split in half by a large peninsula. This strip of land used to be the ridge between Bear Gutter Creek and The Bronx River. The original road from Armonk to

Kensico village ran its length. The now off-limits area is rumored to have old foundations of homes that once proudly stood in Kensico.

The area's flooding reduced the once mighty Archer's Hill that triumphantly stood over the quiet farming village into an island. Rumored to be littered with old wagon trails and stone foundations of homes that belonged to Kensico residents, Westchester County's largest island spans 723 acres, earning its name, Great Island.

Some believe this off-limits location is the burial place of the village's namesake, Sachem **Cockenseco**, and the grave site of Sachem Pathungo. Legend says the mighty Siwanoy's former leader cursed the land after its inhabitants betrayed his trust by destroying trees designated as off-limits.

The former steep hilltop remains covered with ash, black birch, maple, hickory, and oak trees standing proudly as they once did in the days of the Siwanoy and Kensico Village, perhaps camouflaging ghosts of the past. Despite numerous tragedies rocking the quiet farming village, whether an ancient curse influenced any events remains unknown. However, New York City's increased need for water may have predetermined Kensico's ultimate fate.

Every minute, 335,000 gallons of fresh mountain water flow into the Kensico Reservoir from the underground outlet of the 17-foot-wide Catskill Aqueduct, moving at a steady rate of two miles per hour toward the northwestern part of the reservoir.

On the reservoir's eastern side, the newer Delaware Aqueduct delivers 599,000 gallons per minute through a larger opening. These two aqueducts provide most of the 30 billion gallons of water that fill the 2,200-acre reservoir, which supplies many Westchester communities and over eight million New York City residents with their drinking water.

During the 1930s, the Westchester County Historical Commission erected a beautiful monument on Route 22, half a mile north of Old Orchard Street.

The marker reads:

Reuben Wright's Mill - Headquarters of General George Washington and other American generals during the Revolutionary War. 1776-80.

The monument, built with a piece of millstone, overlooks the reservoir and offers passer-byers an opportunity to remember the past.

While some may dismiss the claim, rumors from local fishermen persist that when the reservoir water levels are low, you can sometimes glimpse the shadowy steeple of Kensico's little Methodist church, surrounded by its never exhumed burial ground, reaching up from the depths.

Additional books from the *Nightmarish Neighborhood* series are available now on Amazon and BarnesAndNoble.com.

For more info, please visit: RightOnDudes.com